ARTBOOKS

FROM CRESCENT MOON
PUBLISHING

Leonardo da Vinci
by James Pearson

Early Netherlandish Painting
by Rosalind Mutter

Memling
By W.H.J. & J.C. Weale

Van Eyck
By J. Cyril M. Weale

Piero della Francesca
by Naomi Haskell

Giovanni Bellini
by Julia Davis

Eric Gill: Nuptials of God
by Anthony Hoyland

*Minimal Art and Artists In the
1960s and After*
by Laura Garrard

*Vincent van Gogh: Visionary
Landscapes*
by Stuart Morris

*Mark Rothko: The Art of
Transcendence*
by Julia Davis

Jasper Johns
by L.M. Poole

Brice Marden
by Laura Garrard

*Frank Stella: American Abstract
Artist*
by James Pearson

*Maurice Sendak and the Art of
Children's Book Illustration*
by L.M. Poole

*Sex in Art: Pornography and
Pleasure in Painting and
Sculpture*
by Cassidy Hughes

The Art of Andy Goldsworthy
by William Malpas

*Andy Goldsworthy: Touching
Nature*
by William Malpas

Andy Goldsworthy In Close-Up
by William Malpas

Andy Goldsworthy In America
by William Malpas

Andy Goldsworthy: Pocket Guide
by William Malpas

The Art of Richard Long
by William Malpas

Richard Long: Pocket Guide
by William Malpas

*Constantin Brancusi: Sculpting the
Essence of Things*
by James Pearson

*Alison Wilding: The Embrace of
Sculpture*
by Susan Quinnell

Erotic Art In the 19th Century
By Cassidy Hughes

Erotic Art In the Renaissance
By Cassidy Hughes

Erotic Art
By Cassidy Hughes

The Erotic Object: Sexuality in Sculpture From Prehistory to the Present Day
by Susan Quinnell

Land Art: A Complete Guide
by William Malpas

Land Art In Close-Up
by William Malpas

Land Art In Great Britain
by William Malpas

Land Art In the U.S.A.
by William Malpas

Installation Art In Close-Up
by William Malpas

Colorfield Painting
by Laura Garrard

Bellini
By James Mason

Botticelli
By Henry Binns

Renaissance In Italy: The Fine Arts
By John Addington Symonds

The Life of Michelangelo Buonarroti
By John Addington Symonds

Michelangelo Buonarroti
By Charles Holroyd

Michelangelo
By Estelle Hurll

Michelangelo
By Romain Rolland

Correggio
By Estelle M. Hurll

Tintoretto
By S.L. Bensusan

Titian: A Collection of Fifteen Pictures
By Estelle M. Hurll

The Earlier Work of Titian
By Claude Phillips

The Later Work of Titian
By Claude Phillips

The Earlier and Later Work of Titian
By Claude Phillips

Bernardino Luini
By James Mason

Perugino
By Selwyn Brinton

Perugino
By George Williamson

Raphael
By Estelle M. Hurll

Raphael
By Paul Konody

Dante Gabriel Rossetti
By Esther Wood

Recollections of Dante Gabriel Rossetti
By T. Hall Caine

Burne-Jones
By A. Lys Baldry

The Whistler Book
By Sadakichi Hartmann

Whistler
By T. Martin Wood

Rodin: The Man and His Art
Edited by Judith Cladel

Rodin
By Rainer Maria Rilke

Auguste Rodin
By Camille Mauclair

Corot
By Sidney Allnutt

Fra Angelico
By Jennie Ellis Keysor

Fra Angelico
By James Mason

Fra Angelico
By J.B. Supino

Aubrey Beardsley
By Robert Ross

The Art of Aubrey Beardsley
By Arthur Symons

Leighton
By Ernest Rhys

Millais
By A. Lys Baldry

The Madonna In Art
By Estelle Hurll

Women In the Fine Arts
By Clara Erskine Clement

The Venetian School of Painting
By Evelyn Phillipps

Boucher
By Haldane McFall

Fragonard
By Haldane McFall

Leonardo da Vinci
By Maurice Brockwell

Famous European Painters
By Sarah Bolton

Great Artists
By Jennie Ellis Keysor

Great Pictures
Edited by Esther Singleton

Knights of Art
By Amy Steedman

Delacroix
By Paul Konody

Ingres
By A.J. Finberg

Goya
By Francis Crastre

Dürer
By Hertbert Furst

Albrecht Dürer
By T. Sturge Moore

Dürer
By M.F. Sweetser

Rembrandt van Rijn
By Malcolm Bell

Rembrandt and His Works
By John Burnet

Rembrandt and His Etchings
By Louis Holman

Rembrandt
By Estelle M. Hurll

Rembrandt
By Josef Israels

Turner
By C. Lewis Hind

Turner
By W. Cosmo Monkhouse

The Art of Katsuhiro Otomo
By Jeremy Robinson

The Art of Masamune Shirow
By Jeremy Robinson

ROSSETTI

ROSSETTI

BY LUCIEN PISSARRO

CRESCENT MOON

First published 1894. This edition © 2024.

Set in Book Antiqua 10 on 14pt.
Designed by Radiance Graphics.

British Library Cataloguing in Publication data

ISBN-13 9781861716408
ISBN-13 9781861710895

CRESCENT MOON PUBLISHING
P.O. Box 1312, Maidstone, Kent, ME14 5XU
Great Britain, www.crmoon.com

CONTENTS

NOTE ON THE TEXT

The text is from *Rossetti* by Lucien Pissaro, published by T. C. & E. C. Jack, London, in 1910.

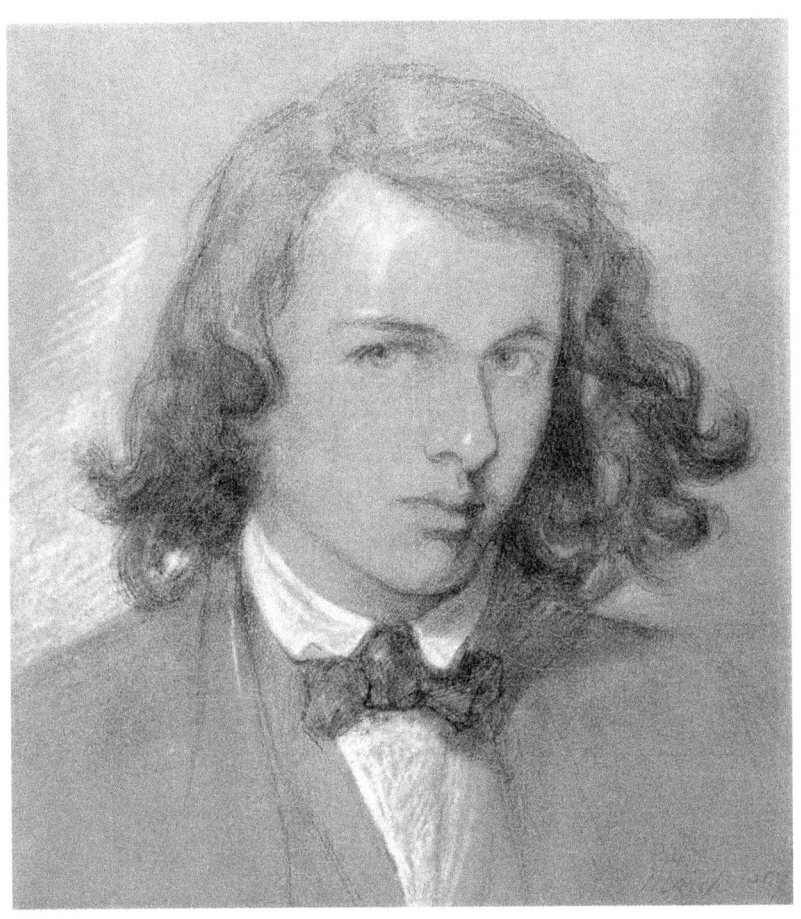

Dante Gabriel Rossetti, Self-Portrait, 1847,
National Portrait Gallery, London

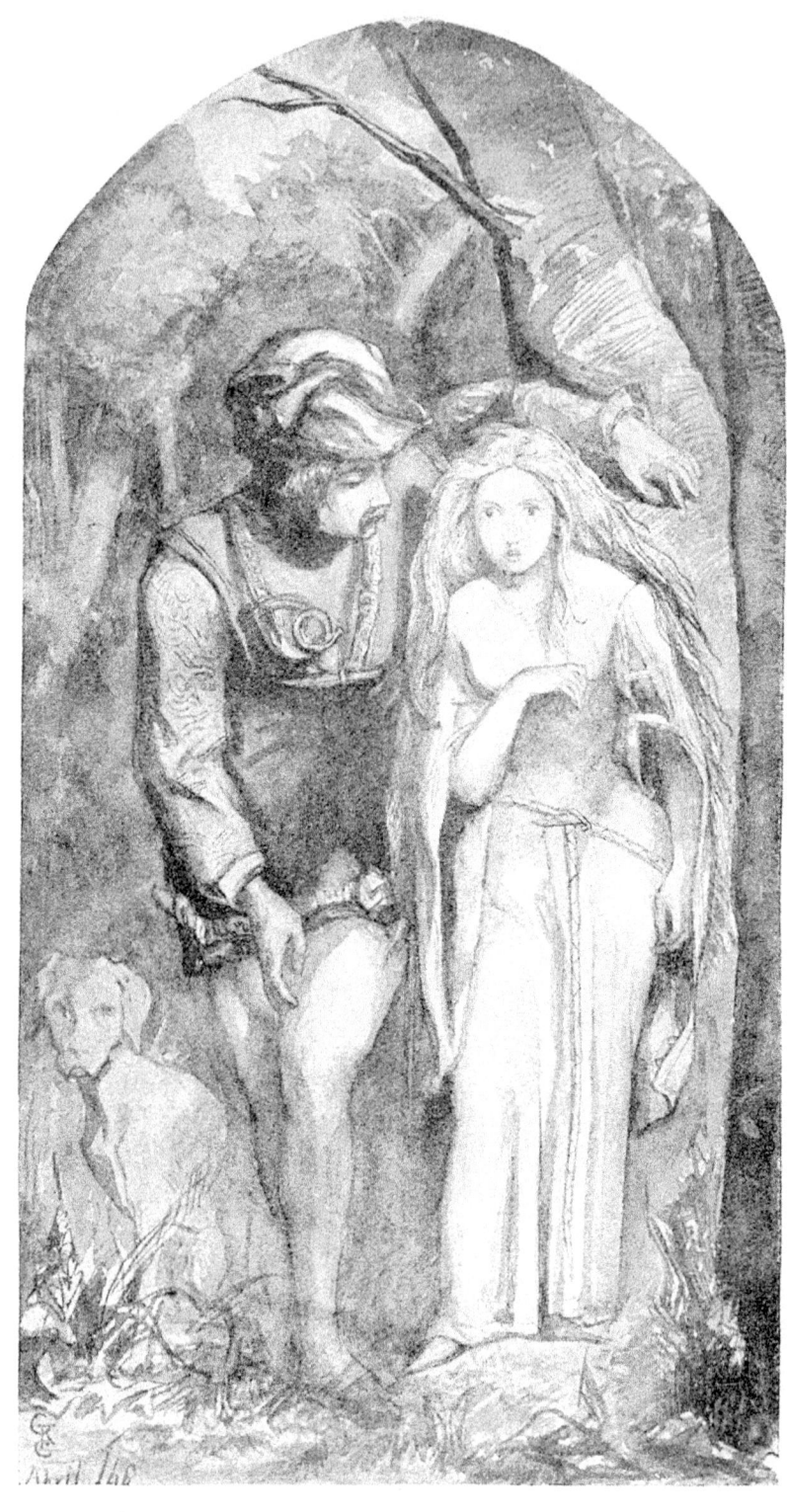

Dante Gabriel Rossetti, La Belle Dame Sans Merci, 1848

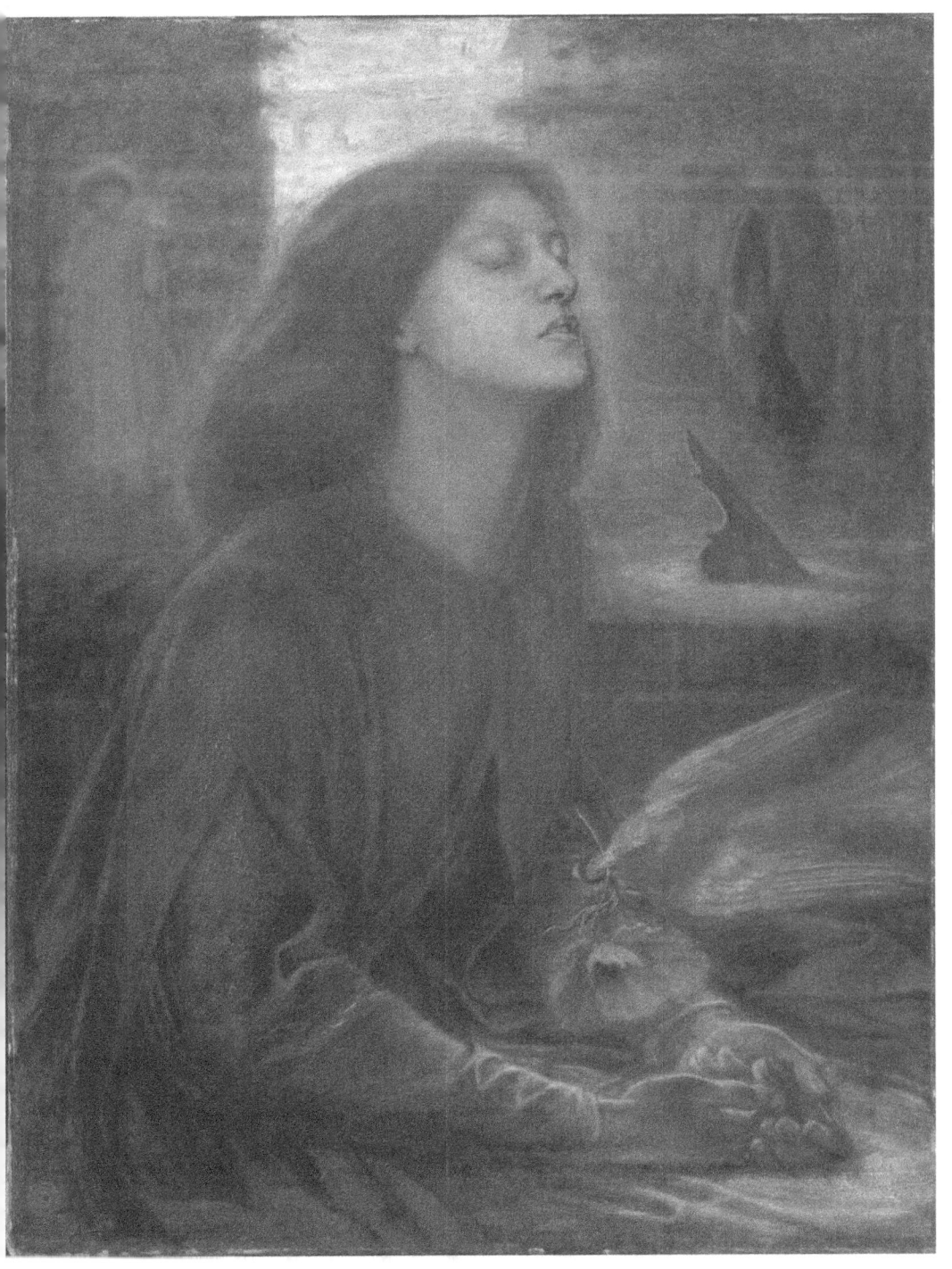

Dante Gabriel Rossetti, Beata Beatrix, 1864-70, Tate Britain

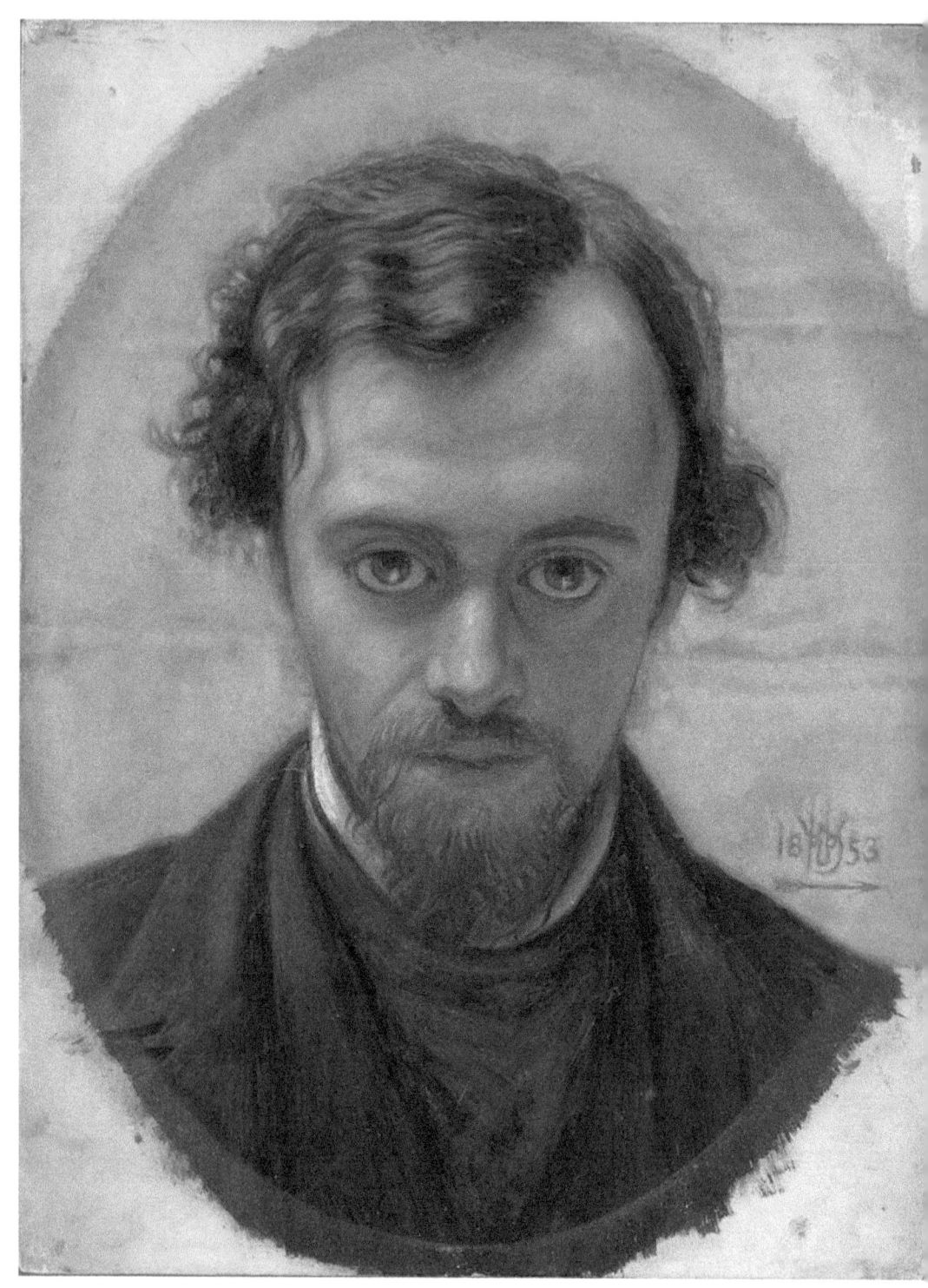

Holman Hunt, Dante Gabriel Rossetti, 1882-83, Birmingham

LIST OF ILLUSTRATIONS IN THE ORIGINAL TEXT

VIII.   Astarte Syriaca
From the Oil Painting in the Manchester Art Gallery

ROSSETTI

I

ABOUT the middle of the nineteenth century Europe woke to the fact that Art, despite its pretention, had lost all touch with tradition and, like a blind man deprived of his staff, stood fumbling for direction. The necessary "point d'appui" took shape in a return to nature. This return was effected by very different means according to the country and artistic milieu in which it occurred. In England it was really a revival of the schools of painting that preceded Raphael and resulted in grafting the complicated passions of our century upon the naïve outlook of the early Italians. The more logical mind of the Frenchman saw that it was not enough to look at nature through the eyes of the Primitives. The point of view had perforce changed and all that it was necessary to borrow from the early schools was the sincerity they brought to the interpretation of phenomena.

We have been told that, in contrast to the continental movement, the realism of the Pre-Raphaelites was applied only to noble subjects. But what is a noble subject? The distinction is a purely literary one. There are no noble subjects in art; there are only harmonies of line and colour.

For example this school would prefer the rose to the cabbage as a subject, on account of the symbols attached to it. It is the Queen of Flowers, the Mystic Rose, &c., &c. But is the rose greater than the cabbage from a purely pictorial point of view? It depends entirely upon how far the painter is able to reveal the beauty, the harmony of form and colour of either. The symbolistic appanage of the rose will not suffice of itself to make a picture, nor for the lack of these symbols may we condemn the cabbage.

The realism of the Pre-Raphaelites developed an absorption in detail, a "bit by bit" painting that was too often detrimental to the whole. In the best works of the early Italians the unity is, in spite of that attention to detail, admirably maintained – in other words the values are preserved. It was not long, however, before Rossetti quitted the path of the Pre-Raphaelites for a broader one. His paintings are entirely symbolistic, therefore literary. Given the personality ofan artist equally gifted as painter and poet, this need not surprise us. Indeed, seeing that Rossetti's pictorial conceptions are exclusively literary, he might be considered as more dominantly a writer than a painter; and this is the light in which he saw himself. We might say he painted "sentiments" and add that sentiment is the property of literature, but in Rossetti's case they have at least the advantage of intensity. They come straight from life, for all his art is more or less connected with the tragedy of his own existence. Herein lies the value of Rossetti's works as artistic creations.

II

Rossetti's family, as his name indicates, was of Italian origin. His ancestors on his father's side belong to Vasto d'Ammone, a small city of the Abruzzi. The original name of the family was Della Guardia. Probably the diminutive Rossetti was given to some red-haired ancestor and retained in spite of the disappearance of that peculiarity. The grandfather of the poet, Dominico Rossetti, was in the iron trade, his son Gabriel Rossetti, born at Vasto, became a custodian of the Bourbon Museum at Naples. He was an ardent patriot and one of the group of reformers who obtained a constitution from Ferdinand, King of the Two Sicilies, in 1820. The return of the King with the Austrian army obliged Gabriel Rossetti, who was compromised by his actions as well as by his patriotic songs, to make his escape from Italy. He did this by the help of the English admiral, commanding the fleet in the bay. Indeed he left Italy disguised in an English uniform.

After passing three years in Malta (1822-1825), he came to England bearing introductions from John Hookham Frere, then Governor of Malta. A year after his arrival he married Frances Mary Livinia Polidori, whose mother was an English lady of the name of Pierce, while her father was Gaetano Polidori, the translator of Milton. Gabriel Rossetti was appointed Professor of Italian literature at King's College in 1831; but owing to the failure of his eyesight he had to resign that position in 1845. He died nine years after, on April 26th, 1854. He is the author of several works, the best known in England are: *Comento analitico sulla Divina Commedia* (1826-1827); *Sullo Spirito Anti-Papale* (1832); and *Il Mistero dell' Amor Platonic* (1840). In Italy, particularly in his own province, his name is held in veneration for services in the cause of liberty. He had four children, the eldest, Maria Francesca, the author of "A Shadow of Dante," died in 1876. Dante Gabriel was the second and was born the 12th of May 1828 at 38 Charlotte Street, Great Portland Place, London. William Michael was the third, and Christina was the youngest.

Very little is known of the early life of Rossetti. He received some instruction at a private school in Foley Street, Portland Place, studying there from the autumn of 1836 to the summer of 1837. He was afterwards sent to King's College School. There he learned Latin, French, and a little Greek. Naturally enough he knew Italian very well from home and also a little German. In his home surroundings the young child's taste for literature was developed very early; at five years old he wrote a drama called "The Slave." Towards his thirteenth year he began a romantic tale in prose, "Roderick and Rosalba." Somewhere about 1843 he wrote a legendary tale entitled "Sir Hugh Le Heron," founded on a tale by Allan Cunningham. His grandfather Gaetano Polidori printed it himself for private circulation, but the work contains no sign of his ultimate development and has been justly omitted from his collected works. Soon the wish to be a painter took possession of Dante Gabriel and, on leaving school, he began his technical education in art at Cary's Academy in Bloomsbury. In 1846 he joined the classes of the Antique School of the Royal Academy. It is worth pointing out that he never followed the Life School of that institution. Conventional methods of study were distasteful to him. He decided to throw up the Academy training and wrote to a painter, not very well known at that date but whose work he admired, asking to be admitted to his studio as a pupil. The painter was Madox Brown, and young Rossetti, given his needs and mode of thought, could not have chosen a more suitable master. Madox Brown was only seven years older than Rossetti, but he had studied at Ghent, Antwerp, Paris, and Rome. He had exhibited some fine cartoons during the early forties for the decoration of the House of Lords. Among these was one that Rossetti had greatly admired at the exhibition of the competitive cartoons in Westminster Hall. It was "Harold's body brought before William the Conqueror." In March 1848 Rossetti entered upon his new experience and Madox Brown agreed to teach him painting, not for a fee but for the mere pleasure of meeting and training a sympathetic spirit. Rossetti did not long remain a regular attendant in the studio. He left after a few months.

On the opening day of the exhibition (May 1848), "Rossetti," says Mr. Hunt, "came up boisterously and in loud tongue made me feel very confused by declaring that mine was the best picture of the year. The fact that it was from Keats ('The Eve of St. Agnes') made him extra enthusiastic, for, I think, no painter had ever before painted from that wonderful poet, who then, it may scarcely be credited, was little known." Rossetti wished so earnestly to become more intimate with Hunt that he agreed to work with him, sharing a studio that the latter had just taken in Cleveland Street, Fitzroy Square. Here he began to paint his first composition, having hitherto done no more than studies, sketches, a number of portraits, some of which reveal excellent work. At this time his literary development was somewhat ahead of his artistic growth. He had already translated the *Vita Nuova* which is alone a monumental achievement, introducing wonderfully into the English the warmth of the southern language; and he had written some of his best known poems, including "The Blessed Damozel," "My Sister's Sleep," "The Portrait," a considerable portion of "Ave," "A last Confession," and the "Bride's Prelude."

Millais and Holman Hunt, whose friendship dated from the Academy Schools, found ground for sympathetic union with Rossetti in their common distaste for contemporary art. They were convinced it was necessary to abandon the conventional style of the day and return to a severe and conscientious study of nature.

They were for a while uncertain as to the path to pursue. Where should they turn for precept and guidance on the line of their new-found principles? Looking through a book of engravings from the Campo Santo of Pisa one day at Millais' house, they thought they had found there the direction they sought. Mr. Holman Hunt tells us that the foundation of the Pre-Raphaelite Brotherhood was the immediate result of coming across the book at that particular time.

While Holman Hunt was painting "Rienzi swearing revenge over his brother's corpse," and Millais, "Lorenzo and Isabella," Rossetti began his "Girlhood of Mary Virgin." As can well be imagined that first composition gave him endless trouble and was the cause of the most violent fits of alternate depression and energy. But the following spring (1849), the three pictures were ready for exhibition. Millais and Hunt were hung in the Royal Academy Exhibition and Rossetti's in the so-called Free Exhibition, which was held in a gallery at Hyde Park Corner. In the "Girlhood of Mary Virgin," he represents a room in the Virgin's home with a balcony on which her father, St. Joachim, is seen tending a vine which grows up towards the top of the picture. On the right, against a dark green curtain, are the figures of St. Anna and the Virgin sitting at an embroidery frame. The mother, in dark green and brown garments with a dull red head-dress, is watching with clasped hands the work in front of her. The young girl, a quite unconventional Madonna dressed in grey, pauses with a needle in her hand gazing in front of her at a child angel holding a white lily. Underneath the pot in which the white lily grows are six big books bearing the names of the six cardinal virtues. The figures, as well as the dove which is perched on the trellis, bear halos, their names being inscribed within. Rossetti painted his mother for St. Anna and his sister Christina for the Virgin. Changing her dark brown hair to golden, he broke a rule of the Brotherhood, which decrees that the artist shall copy his model most scrupulously. The picture was signed with his name, followed by the three letters P.R.B. Rossetti having revealed the meaning of these three letters to a friend it was soon generally known and no peace was given to those who dared to stand up against traditional authority. It is necessary to explain that, at that time, Raphael was considered the greatest of all painters. All who came before him were ignored and a set of fixed rules supposed to have been deduced from his work was taught in all the schools. The revolt of the "Brethren" was directed much more against those rules than against Raphael's work which, in all probability, they hardly knew.

At about the same time that he painted "Mary's Girlhood," Rossetti did a portrait in oils of his father, his first work of this kind. He also drew an outline design of a lute player and his lady, a subject taken from Coleridge's "Genevieve"; a pen-and-ink drawing of "Gretchen in the Chapel," with Mephistopheles whispering in her ear, and "The Sun may shine and we be cold," a sketch of a girl near a window, apparently a prisoner. To this period also belongs the important pen-and-ink drawing, "Il Saluto di Beatrice," representing in two parts the meeting of Dante and Beatrice, first in a street of Florence and secondly in Paradise.

The most important of Rossetti's Pre-Raphaelite work during the two years following 1848 is the "Ecce Ancilla Domini," quite in keeping in sentiment with the picture of the previous year. Both these pictures are a little timid in treatment. In the "Ecce Ancilla Domini," the Virgin clad in white is sitting on her bed, as if just awakened, and sees with awe the full length of an angel, also clad in white, floating in front of her and holding a white lily in his hand. The walls are white but there is a blue curtain behind the Virgin's head and a red embroidery on its frame is standing in the foreground at the foot of the bed. The drapery of the angel is a little stiff and the whole effect rather hard, but notwithstanding this youthful fault the whole work is restrained and full of charm both in drawing and colour.

This picture was exhibited in 1850 at the same Free Exhibition, which was moved this year from Hyde Park Corner to Portland Place.

The Pre-Raphaelites were now attacked by the press still more fiercely than before, but they found a champion in Ruskin who took up their defence in a series of letters to the *Times*, and in so doing laid down an elaborate statement of principles. Thus it came about that the broad and possibly nebulous ideas of the Brethren became transmuted into hard and fast rules, which the young painters had to accept, partly out of gratitude to their benefactor, partly because they agreed with them. Rossetti painted only three pictures strictly according to the Pre-Raphaelite rules. Curiously enough the best genuine Pre-Raphaelite picture is "Work" by Ford Madox Brown, who not believing in cliques refused to join the group.

Round Rossetti were grouped his brother, William Michael, his sister Christina, with Woolner, Collinson, Deverell, Millais, Hunt, Madox Brown, William Bell Scott, and Coventry Patmore. Of all these Hunt and Millais alone showed no inclination for writing. The group naturally formed a school of literary thought of which "The Germ," originated by Rossetti to propagate the ideas of the P.R.B., was the outcome.

The cumbrous title "Monthly Thoughts in Literature, Poetry, and Art," was first intended to be the title of this special publication of the brotherhood, but at a meeting held in Rossetti's studio, 72 Newman Street, in December 1849, when the first number was just ready for publication it was decided to change the name for the simple title "The Germ." This was proposed by Mr. Cave Thomas, an intimate friend of the group.

To the first number Rossetti contributed "My Sister's Sleep," and a prose romance "Hand and Soul." Following numbers contained "The Blessed Damozel," "The Carillon," "Sea limits" (under the title "From the Cliffs"), and several sonnets. Only the first two numbers of the publication were called "The Germ." The publication was known as "Art and Poetry" in the third and fourth issues.

"The Germ," as its short career showed, did not meet with success, but it served to establish Rossetti's reputation among a small group of artists and admirers. Rossetti's literary contributions were far more matured than his paintings and it is surprising that they did not attract more attention. "Hand and Soul" is specially valuable as bearing a record of psychological experiences which gives a clear glimpse of Rossetti's mind.

III

The storm of abuse caused by his two first pictures assisted a natural inclination to give up his first source of religio-mystical inspiration. Gradually the young painter groped his way towards romantic subjects and discovered a rich mine of them in the works of Browning, Dante, Keats, and the "Morte d'Arthur" of Malory. He may be said to have found there the subjects of most of his compositions, and his works inspired by these poets are delightfully full of originality and ingenuity.

He tried first a large canvas from the page's song in "Pippa Passes" but had to abandon it. The composition of it remains in a little painting called "Hist, said Kate the Queen," dated 1851. He executed two other pen-and-ink designs from Browning entitled "Taurellos' first sight of Fortune" and the "Laboratory," at about the same time. Probably the latter was his first essay in water-colour, it is very different from those for which he is popularly known.

In "Beatrice at the Wedding Feast, denying her salutation to Dante," a small water-colour of 1849 from the "Vita Nuova," the central figure is a portrait of Miss Elizabeth Siddal who became acquainted with Rossetti at about this date. She was the daughter of a Sheffield cutler and was working in a milliner's shop. Walter Deverell discovered her one day, when he was shopping with his mother. He persuaded her to sit for him for his "Viola" and later to Rossetti. Her portrait can be seen in a picture by Holman Hunt and in Millais' Ophelia. Miss Siddal sat for most of the women in Rossetti's earliest and finest water-colours.

To 1851 belongs the beautiful little composition called "Borgia," in which Lucrezia can be seen dressed in an ample white gown brightened all over with coloured ribbons and bows, sitting with a lute in her hands. In the foreground two children are dancing. Leaning over her left shoulder is the Pope Alexander VI., while her brother Cæsar stands on the other side beating time with a knife against a wine-glass on the table.

Rossetti was not long in discovering that Miss Siddal had a strong aptitude for art. With his special gift of influencing others the position of model was soon merged into that of a pupil. Under his guidance Miss Siddal made rapid progress and her water-colours show a fine sense of colour.

The sympathy between artist and pupil ripened into affection. The exact date of their engagement is not known, but it was probably in 1853, certainly not later than 1854, and was at first kept secret at Miss Siddal's request.

To the year 1854 belongs the water-colour, "King Arthur's Tomb," in which Lancelot and Guenevere are seen bidding farewell over the tomb of King Arthur; and to the following year belong the three water-colours, "The Nativity," "La Belle Dame Sans Merci," and the "Annunciation," as well as the drawing for a wood-cut, illustrating a poem called "The Maids of Elfen-Mere" by William Allingham.

The artistic and romantic force which had produced the Pre-Raphaelite movement had another important work to do five or six years later, when a fusion of two movements took place: the early Pre-Raphaelites represented by Rossetti, Holman Hunt, and Millais, joined the later movement inaugurated by Morris and Burne-Jones. The second of these groups originated at Exeter College, Oxford. It took shape like the first one in a revolt against the Art formulæ of the age. The Oxford group, like the P.R.B., had a magazine to express their views.

At Christmas 1855 Burne-Jones came up to London and was introduced to Rossetti, whom he and Morris admired greatly. Rossetti contributed "The Burden of Nineveh," and a little altered version of "The Blessed Damozel" to the "Oxford and Cambridge Magazine," the organ of William Morris.

One year later Burne-Jones and Morris settled in London in rooms at 17 Red Lion Square. Both young men were soon completely under Rossetti's influence, and their studio became a sort of centre for all members of his circle. There, in order to furnish and decorate these rooms, the first essays in designing furniture were made. Rossetti painted a pair of panels for a cabinet. He made use of the subject of his early pen-and-ink drawing, "The Salutation of Beatrice," representing, in two divisions, Dante meeting Beatrice in Florence and again in Paradise, with a figure of Love standing between them in the midst of symbols. Besides those panels Rossetti painted on the backs of two arm-chairs, "Gwendolen in the Witch-tower" and the "Arming of a Knight," both subjects from poems by William Morris.

To 1857 belongs the charming series of water-colours acquired by William Morris: "The Damsel of the St. Grael," "The Death of Breuse sans pitié," "The Chapel before the Lists," "The Tune of Seven Towers," and "The Blue Closet." The two last were special favourites with Morris who used their romantic titles for two of his poems. This year also, he painted the "Wedding of St. George," "The Gate of Memory," "The Garden Bower," and a "Christmas Carol."

During the vacation of 1857 Rossetti went to Oxford with Morris to visit the architect, Benjamin Woodward, who was constructing a debating-hall for the Union Society. Rossetti saw an opportunity for mural decoration, and arrangements were made with the building committee in charge that seven artists including Rossetti, Burne-Jones, and Morris, should undertake the decoration gratuitously, the Union only defraying their expenses at Oxford and providing all necessary material. Rossetti took for subjects, "Launcelot asleep before the Chapel of the Sanc Grael" and "Sir Galahad, Sir Bors, and Sir Percival, receiving the Sanc Grael." Before the pictures were finished they began to fade, the walls having been badly prepared and Rossetti's designs were never completed.

While at Oxford, in the summer of 1857, at the theatre, Rossetti was very much impressed one night by the striking beauty of Miss Burden, the daughter of an Oxford resident. He obtained an introduction in order to ask for sittings. A pen-and-ink head called "Queen Guinevere," probably meant to replace the earlier studies done for "Launcelot at the Shrine," was the first result of the new acquaintance. Several years later, after the death of his wife, Miss Burden, then Mrs. William Morris, again sat to Rossetti for several of his important pictures.

IV

On the 23rd of May 1860, the long delayed marriage of Rossetti to Miss Siddal took place in St. Clement's Church, Hastings, and the married couple went to Paris for their honeymoon. While staying there Rossetti did two pen-and-ink drawings one of which called "How they meet themselves," was done to replace the one made in 1851 and lost; the other representing a scene from the "Life of Johnson" by Boswell, quite an unusual subject for the artist. To the same year belongs the picture representing Lucrezia Borgia washing her hands after preparing poison for her husband the Duke Alphonso of Bisceglia.

In 1861 Rossetti's translation from the Italian poets was at last published with the "Vita Nuova" in a volume entitled "The Italian Poets from Cuillo d'Alcamo to Dante Alighieri (1100, 1200, 1300)." The painter poet was enabled to publish this book through Messrs. Smith, Elder & Co. by the generous assistance of Ruskin who advanced £100 to the publisher, but the sale of the first edition was only just sufficient to pay that sum back, leaving a balance of about £10 to the author. He proposed to etch for the frontispiece a charming design of which various pen-and-ink versions exist, but being displeased with the plate he destroyed it. In the same year he painted a small portrait of his wife called "Regina Cordium." The head with ruddy hair hanging loose on the shoulders against a gold background, fills nearly all the canvas and a hand is seen on the left side of the picture holding a pansy. More than one replica of that portrait exists, and several heads from different sitters are called "Regina Cordium." Another important production of the year is "Cassandra." The subject is a scene on the walls of Troy before Hector's last battle. He has been warned in vain by the prophetess, who is seen leaning against a pillar, tearing her clothes in despair. Hector is rushing down the steps, and the whole composition is full of soldiers, every space being filled with some incident related to the central subject, giving that aspect of concentrated composition so special to Rossetti.

The two years following his marriage (1860-1862) were amongst the most prolific of Rossetti's life both in ideas and invention. Besides "Cassandra" he planned the composition for a large picture which was commissioned but never finished, representing Perseus with the Medusa's head; and he made the first pencil studies for his famous "Beata Beatrix."

With 1862 is associated the water-colour, "Bethlehem Gate." It is also about this time (1861-1862) that the now famous firm of Morris, Marshall, Faulkner & Co. was established with the co-operation of William Morris, Faulkner, Burne-Jones, Madox Brown, Webb, and others as active members.

The idea of the commercial attempt on the artistic lines to reform the art of decoration and furniture-making was, says Mr. Mackail, largely due to Madox Brown, but perhaps more to Rossetti, who, in spite of his artistic qualities, was a very good business man and had the scent of a trained financier for anything likely to pay. The little band of original artists and designers took in hand tapestry, furniture, wall papers, stained-glass, and later on, carpet weaving and dyeing. The terms under which they worked were very simple. Each member was to be paid for the work commissioned by the firm, and the profits were to be divided in a proper ratio at the end.

The new firm had plenty to do owing to the demand for ritual decorations caused by the Anglo-Catholic movement. Amongst the first commissions were those for adorning two new churches then being built – St. Martin-on-the-Hill, Scarborough, and St. Michael at Brighton. For the first one Rossetti made a design for two pulpit panels and several windows.

In dealing with stained-glass Rossetti who was specially gifted as a decorator, understood his medium, and in making his design took into account all the limitations of the material. He did not seek to paint a picture on glass, but maintained that idea of a mosaic of coloured-glass that is seen to so much advantage in the early *vitraux*.

Amongst works designed by him for the firm Morris & Co. the following may be mentioned: "Adam and Eve," two designs for stained-glass, and "St. George and the Dragon," six designs for stained-glass. One of them representing the princess drawing the fatal lot he painted as a water-colour. "King Rene's Honeymoon," a design for one of four panels representing the Arts, was done for a gothic cabinet that Mr. J. P. Seddon ordered from Morris & Co. Rossetti's design for "Music" shows the king bent over a chamber-organ kissing his bride while she is playing. He designed also one of the minor panels "Gardening." There is a water-colour of the same subject under the title of "Spring." "Amor, Amans, Amata," were three small figures in ovals, done for the back of a sofa, which Rossetti had made for himself. He kept it for many years in his house at Chelsea. "Sir Tristran and la Belle Iseult drinking the Love potion" was a fine design intended to be one of a series of stained-glass windows. "King Rene's Honeymoon" was done for a series of stained-glass windows. "The Annunciation" is a design for a window, quite different from the early version of the same subject. "Threshing" is a design for a glazed tile. "The Sermon on the Mount" was done for a memorial window in Christ Church, Albany Street, erected in 1869 to the memory of his aunt, Miss Polidori.

In either 1861 or 1862 Rossetti designed two illustrations for his sister Christina's book of poems "Goblin Market." They were engraved on wood and appear in Messrs. Macmillan's edition.

In May 1861 Mrs. Rossetti gave birth to a still-born child. Her recovery was slow, and this trouble did not improve her consumptive tendencies. She suffered, too, from a very severe form of neuralgia, for which laudanum was prescribed.

On the night of the 11th of February 1862 she took an overdose and Rossetti, returning home from lecturing at the Working Men's College, found her dying. In a terrible state of anxiety, after seeking one doctor after another, he called in Madox Brown for help, but all in vain. The following morning his wife died, after only two years of married life. The grief of Rossetti was overwhelming and the touching scene in which he buried the manuscript of his poems with his beloved wife has been told many a time.

V

After this tragic event Rossetti could no longer live in the rooms
he had occupied at Chatham Place. He looked for some others,
living meanwhile for a few months in a house in Lincoln's Inn
Fields. Then he took a lease of the house at No. 16 Cheyne Walk,
sharing it at first with Swinburne and Meredith. Mr. Meredith did
not stay long and after awhile Mr. Swinburne also gave up his
tenancy, leaving Rossetti sole occupant of the premises.

One of the last works he did before his misfortune, and the
last picture for which his wife sat to him, was the water-colour of
"St. George and the Princess Sabra." For sometime after the blow
of his wife's death he was idle. The first things he did after his
recovery was a crayon portrait of his mother (1862) followed by
"The Girl at a Lattice," "Joan of Arc," and a replica of his early
"Paolo and Francesca."

The celebrated picture of "Beata Beatrix," now in the Tate
Gallery is dated 1863, but was finished later, being only partly
painted in that year. In Rossetti's own words the following is a
description of the picture: "The picture illustrates the *Vita Nuova*,
embodying symbolically the death of Beatrice as treated in that
work. The picture is not intended at all to represent death, but to
render it under the semblance of a trance in which Beatrice,
seated at a balcony overlooking the city, is suddenly rapt from
earth to heaven...."

The whole strikes a sombre note apart from its symbolic representation through its delicious purple harmony. The city in the sunset light in the distance, supposed to be Florence, is very like London in atmospheric effect. Beatrice is seen sitting at the balcony against the sunset background, with the light playing round her golden auburn hair, in fashion suggesting an aureole. She is dressed in green with dull purple sleeves. A bright red bird holding in its beak a dim purple poppy, emblem of death, is flying towards her. In the misty distance the figures of Dante and Love are watching her. Rossetti painted in 1872 a replica of that picture, adding to the main subject the meeting of Dante and Beatrice in Paradise, with maidens bearing instruments of music. He was rather reluctant to send out that replica, but the unwillingness was overcome. He painted several others, none of them being equal in quality to the original.

In 1863 Rossetti painted an oil picture called "Helen of Troy," and the last of the St. George subjects, representing St. George killing the dragon, which is a water-colour version of the stained-glass series. Then come three small subjects, "Belcolore," a girl in a circular frame biting a rosebud. Of this there is a red chalk study and a water-colour version, "Brimfull," a water-colour showing a lady stooping to sip from a full glass, and a picture called "A Lady in Yellow."

Rossetti now gave up painting those quaint little romantic subjects so intense in literary feeling and dramatic expression, and devoted himself to large single figures upon a background of rich accessories.

When a painter makes a single figure the central interest of his picture, he must, to a certain extent, avail himself of psychological facts in the model before him, for if he recognises no limits to the foreign sentiment and character he may impose, he will, little by little, fall to the creation of a type which is not far short of a monstrosity. Although the first of his pictures in this new style are among his finest works we see this inevitable degeneration in Rossetti's latest paintings.

The first pictures of this kind and some of the best are, "Fazio's Mistress," and "Lady Lilith." The former is dated 1863, but was altered and repainted ten years later, and Rossetti changed its title to "Aurelia." In 1864 he painted the latter which is a modern conception of that first wife of Adam mentioned in the old Talmudic Legend. The Lady Lilith is seated against a background covered with roses. Dressed in white, she holds a mirror in her hand, and combs her long fair hair. Although dated 1864 it was really not finished until 1867. The face as it is now was repainted in 1873 from a different model, and is said to be quite inferior to the former one. Rossetti at that time seemed to be a victim of a mania for repainting his earlier work.

The next great picture, begun in 1864, is "Venus Verticordia," the oil version of which was not finished before 1868. It represents the nude bust of a massively built woman surrounded by roses and honeysuckle. She holds an arrow in her right hand and in the left an apple on which a yellow butterfly has alighted. The face is conventionally pretty and lacks character.

"Morning Music," an elaborate little water-colour; "Monna Pomona," a girl holding an apple with roses on her lap and in a basket at her side; "How Sir Galahad, Sir Bors, and Sir Percival received the Holy Grael" (done in his earlier manner); "Roman de la Rose," a water-colour version of the earlier panel, and "The Madness of Ophelia," represent the remaining production of 1864.

There is little to mention in 1865. The most important productions of that year were "The Blue Bower," and "The Merciless Lady." In the "Merciless Lady," a water-colour in the style of his earlier romantic manner, a man sits on a bank of turf between two maidens, with a sunlit meadow behind. He seems attracted by the one on his left who is fair and plays a lute, the other, his lady love, holds his hand and with a sad expression tries to win him back to her. "A Fight for a Woman," the composition of which is of a very early date, and the oil-painting, "Bella e Buona," but renamed "Il Ramoscello," were also painted in 1865.

After these came "The Beloved," finished in 1866, but worked again in 1873, this time without being spoiled. In writing to the owner of this picture Rossetti said: "I mean it to be like jewels," and he carried out his intention. In the middle of the picture is the fair-haired bride radiant in rich stuffs, her gown is green, with large sleeves embroidered in gold and red. She is surrounded by four dark-haired maidens, on the foreground a little negro, adorned with a head-band and a necklace showing the beautiful invention of Rossetti's taste in decorative art, is holding a golden vase of roses.

Next comes the "Monna Vanna," which represents a lady dressed in a magnificent embroidered robe with large sleeves, holding a fan of black and yellow plumes. Her luxuriant hair is falling from each side of her face on to her shoulders, a bunch of roses is seen in a vase on the left top corner of the picture.

"The Sibylla Palmifera," and "Monna Vanna," were not completed before 1870. The latter represents a Sibyl sitting underneath a stone canopy, which is carved on one side with a cupid's head wreathed with roses, and on the other with a skull crowned with red poppies. The Sibyl is clad in crimson, her brown hair is parted and falling each side of her face, a green coif spreads from her head over her shoulder and she holds a palm-leaf in her hand. There is a replica of the head of "Sibylla Palmifera." In the same year (1866) he painted in oils a portrait of his mother, and made a large crayon drawing of his sister Christina. He also made two illustrations for her volume of poems, "The Prince's Progress."

In 1867 Rossetti painted in oils "The Christmas Carol," of which a crayon study exists; "Monna Rosa," and the "Loving Cup." For the water-colour, "The Return of Tibullus to Delia," there are numerous sketches made from Miss Siddal sitting on a couch biting a tress of her hair, which show that the design must have been of a much earlier date. The water-colours, "Aurora," "Tessa la Bionda;" the crayons, "Magdalene," "Peace," "Contemplation," and the crayon replica, "Venus Verticordia," bear the same date.

Unfortunately about this time Rossetti began to have serious trouble with his eyesight, and had probably to reduce his hours of work. All the same in 1868 he painted a portrait of Mrs. Morris, who has kindly lent it to the Tate Gallery, where it can now be seen. Several chalk crayon studies have been done for this portrait. Then he began the picture of "The Daydream," representing Mrs. Morris sitting on the lower branches of a sycamore tree, a replica in water-colour of "Bocca Baciate," called "Bionda del Balcone"; "The Rose," a water-colour; a crayon drawing, "Aurea Catena," some studies for "La Pia," which was begun about this time, and a water-colour replica of "Venus Verticordia."

Rossetti had now reached his fortieth year and for about a twelvemonth had been suffering from insomnia. This was the cause of the break-up of his health, for to gain relief he acquired the habit of taking chloral, a drug of which the properties were then little known.

VI

During a visit to Penkill the thought of publishing his early poems occurred to him. Towards the end of 1869 he was busy with their preparation. Some of them were in circulation in manuscript in a more or less finished condition and some others were buried with his wife. As a relief from the strain of painting he began to write again. "The Ballad of Troy Town," part of "Eden Bower," and the "Stream's Secret," were among the new poems. He thought at first to collect as many of the earlier works as he could remember, together with those of which friends had manuscript copies, and to have them set up in type as the foundation of a possible volume. But he was persuaded with difficulty to apply for permission to open the grave of his wife in order to recover the buried manuscript. In 1870 the book, under the title, "Poems by Dante Gabriel Rossetti," was published by Mr. F. S. Ellis, then in King Street, Covent Garden. Round Rossetti and his buried poems a sort of legend had been growing up which, aided by his fame as a painter, guarded his work against the indifference with which a volume of verses by an unknown poet is bound to be received. The book proved a great success and within a week or two Rossetti found himself in possession of £300.

This success was not achieved without raising some jealousy. Mr. Buchanan, under the pseudonym of "Thomas Maitland" rushed into print with the damning essay that appeared in the *Contemporary Review* for October 1871, under the title "The Fleshly School of Poetry." This attack was repeated by the same writer in a pamphlet. Rossetti in ill health and suffering from nervous fancies, considered that there was a conspiracy against him, a view that, had his health been stronger, he would not perhaps have adopted. The publication of the article aggravated his insomnia. Dr. Gordon Hake offered him his house at Roehampton in order to procure a change for the sufferer, who either by accident or of set purpose had taken the contents of a phial of laudanum, and lay for two days between life and death. Prompt treatment, and his strong constitution helped recovery. He was taken to Scotland where he resumed work on a replica of "Beata Beatrix." Out-of-door exercise, early hours, and absence of worries, helped a great deal to bring about his partial recovery. In September 1872 he left Scotland and went to Kelmscott where he shared a fine Elizabethan manor house with William Morris.

His work during 1872-1874 consisted mostly in repainting many of his earlier pictures. He worked again on "Lilith," "Beloved," "Monna Vanna," and others. In July 1874 he left Kelmscott and came back to London, never to return to the quiet manor house, which from this time was in possession of Morris alone.

Besides retouching his earlier work during the time of his stay at Kelmscott, Rossetti started a number of new canvases, and made a certain number of studies for use in future work. Among them are: "Rosa Triplex," three heads from the same sitter, Miss May Morris. This drawing is one of four or five versions. A portrait in red chalk on grey-green paper of Mrs. W. J. Stillman, "La Donna de la Fiamma," and "Silence," probably studies for pictures never painted, the little head of a lady holding a small branch of rose-leaves called "Rose-leaf." "Mariana," an oil painting, its title taken from a scene of "Measure for Measure," and "A Lady with a Fan," being a portrait of Mrs. Schott, were all prepared about this time. He also started the first studies for his big picture, "Dante's Dream," among them a study from Mrs. Morris for the head of the dead Beatrice, a head of Dante, and studies for the two maidens holding the pall. "Troy Town," after his own ballad, and "The Death of Lady Macbeth," are two designs for pictures never painted. "Pandora" was completed in 1871. "Water Willow," a portrait of Mrs. Morris is specially interesting because the river landscape behind represents Kelmscott. A coloured chalk study for that picture exists, the only difference between the portrait and the study being that the background of the latter represents a river without the view of Kelmscott. The "Dante's Dream" begun in 1870 was finished towards the end of 1871. It is the largest picture Rossetti ever painted, the subject is that of the early water-colour of 1856, and the picture illustrates the following:

> "Then Love spoke thus: 'Now all shall be made clear;
> Come and behold our lady where she lies.'
> • • •
> Then carried me to see my lady dead;
> And standing at her head
> Her ladies put a veil over her;
> And with her was such very humbleness
> That she appeared to say, 'I am at peace.'"

In the composition Dante is led by Love to where Beatrice lies dead, and Love bends down to kiss her. On either side of the bier where she lies, two maidens dressed in green are holding a pall covered with May flowers and the floor is strewed with poppies, emblem of death. On each side of the picture there are winding staircases through which one sees the sunny streets of Florence. Love is dressed in flame colour and birds of the same hue are flying about to suggest that the place is filled with the Spirit of Love.

Proserpine was the next picture Rossetti undertook. It was begun on four canvases. The fourth when finished was sold. Rossetti, who at that time had assistants to help him in making the replicas of his earlier work, painted to satisfy the demand of his patrons, and much controversy raged round this picture. It is impossible to say if it was entirely painted by him, but he owned to it although it was not a good one. The purchaser was dissatisfied so he agreed to take it back. The three unfinished versions were cut down and transformed into heads, one of which, with the adding of some floral accessories, and a slight change in the hands, was called "Blanziflore" or "Snowdrops." One cannot help being a little puzzled by the notion of beginning four canvases of the same picture at the same time, it suggests too much of the commercial spirit.

In 1872 "Veronica Veronese," and the "Bower Meadow," were painted, the former illustrating the following lines, supposed to be a quotation taken from Girolamo Ridolfi's letters which are inscribed on the frame:

"Se penchant vivement la Véronica jeta les premières notes sur la feuille vierge. Ensuite elle prit l'archet du violon pour réaliser son rêve; mais avant de décrocher l'instrument suspendu, elle resta quelques instants immobile en écoutant l'oiseau inspirateur, pendant que sa main gauche errait sur les cordes cherchant le motif suprême encore éloigné. C'était le mariage des voix de la nature et de l'âme – l'aube d'une création mystique."

The Lady Veronica, dressed in green, is sitting in front of a little table on which is her music manuscript. Behind her on the left-hand top corner is a canary perched on a cage and at her side stands a glass of daffodils. She is leaning forward as if listening to the bird, plucking with her left hand the strings of a violin hanging on the wall in front of her while she holds the bow in her right hand.

The "Bower Meadow" represents two women playing instruments and two dancing figures, for which he made charming crayon studies. All these figures were painted on an old background study of trees and foliage he had painted in 1850, in his Pre-Raphaelite days when he was working with Holman Hunt.

The next great oil canvas is dated 1873, and is called "The

Ghirlandata." To this year belongs "Ligeia Siren," a drawing of a sea-maiden playing on a musical instrument, a preliminary study for "Sea Spell."

"The Damsel of the Sanc Grael" was painted in 1874; it is a second version of that subject strangely showing the psychological change in Rossetti. The primitive simplicity so characteristic of the mediæval legend and also of his early work has disappeared. The austere damsel has become a "pretty" girl, with fair flowing hair, who holds a goblet. The unfinished "Boat of Love" was also begun in 1874. Rossetti came back to London in that year as has already been stated.

The dissolution of the firm Morris, Marshall, Faulkner & Co. took place at that time and was reconstituted under the sole management of Morris. The dissolution did not take place without a certain amount of friction, caused by the disagreement between Morris and Brown. Rossetti seems to have taken Brown's part, and although Rossetti and Morris did not quarrel, they saw very little of one another from that date. But it is well to remember that Rossetti lived a very secluded life, seeing very few people and labouring under the delusion that a widespread conspiracy existed against him. This was apparently one of the hallucinations resulting from the habitual use of chloral.

The end of 1875 and beginning of 1876 were passed first in a house at Bognor and after at a friend's in Hampshire. The artist was then working on his pictures, "The Blessed Damozel," "The Spirit of the Rainbow," and "Forced Music."

In 1877 serious illness kept him two months in bed, and when better he was taken to a little cottage near Herne Bay. There he was able to resume his work and drew a crayon group of his mother and sister as well as two separate drawings of his sister and one of his mother. To that year belongs the "Astarte Syriaca" (now in the Corporation Art Gallery of Manchester). The Syrian Venus stands against a red sunset sky in which the moon is rising, gazing full face, with large dreamy eyes. On the right and left two angel figures, holding torches, look upwards.

In that year the Grosvenor Gallery was founded and Madox Brown, Rossetti, and Burne-Jones were asked to exhibit. Madox Brown and Rossetti refused, but Burne-Jones accepted. The exhibition of his work there brought him the enormous popularity he enjoyed. Down to that time the public curiosity which had been roused by the controversies following the forming of the P.R.B. had not been satisfied.

VII

After 1877 Rossetti kept strictly to his house at 16 Cheyne Walk visited only by a few faithful friends.

He began to write again in 1878. By March 1881 he had enough material for a new volume, "Ballads and Sonnets," the MS. of which was offered to and accepted by Messrs. Ellis & White on the same terms as his first book, now out of print after running into a sixth edition. The "Ballads and Sonnets" met with quite as great success as the earlier volume, this time without any discordant note of criticism. In this year Rossetti sold his great picture of "Dante's Dream" to the Corporation of Liverpool.

The two finished works of 1878 are: "A Vision of Fiametta," and a water-colour called "Bruna Brunelleschi." To that year must be added the unfinished design called "Desdemona's Death Song," various studies for the figure of Desdemona, a design of the entire composition done on a scale about half-life size, as well as a beginning of the picture on canvas, which was not continued. The Faust subject that he intended to paint, "Gretchen, or Risen at Dawn," was not more advanced. As time went on and his health failed his output diminished.

In 1879 Rossetti painted a replica of the "Blessed Damozel" with its predella, changing the background of lovers and substituting two angels' heads. "La Donna de la Fenestra" was also completed in that year.

In 1880 and 1881 Rossetti was working on three large pictures, "The Day Dream," "The Salutation of Beatrice," and "La Pia," as well as on "Found," the early attempt at a modern subject that he was never able to finish. He painted several replicas, the most important being a smaller version of "Dante's Dream." The "Daydream" begun in 1868 was also completed at this time and the picture has since been given to the South Kensington Museum by its owner Mr. Ionidès. "The Salutation of Beatrice" is quite different from the earlier design of the same name and shows those defects of his later work that we have pointed out; it was not quite finished at the time of his death. "La Pia" is the last picture painted and shows the same faults as the last mentioned.

In September 1881 Rossetti went for a trip in the lake district of Cumberland accompanied by Mr. Hall Caine, but after a month his health grew worse and he returned in haste to London. A few days later he became so ill that he required very careful nursing. After a partial recovery from this illness he was once more interrupted in his work by an attack of nervous paralysis, which seized him suddenly. This last attack was due to the chloral he had been in the habit of taking for so long and it was then strictly forbidden. The habit of so many years was not to be broken without much discomfort and suffering, but he gradually got better. As soon as he was well enough he was taken to Birchington-on-Sea in February 1882, there he managed to work a little, but was soon attacked by an old disorder, and in his weakened state of health he could not throw it off. He grew weaker and worse. Death came with the 10th of April 1882, and the painter poet is buried in the little churchyard of Birchington.

In the last days of his life, when he could paint no more, he made an attempt to finish the story of "St. Agnes of Intercession" which was begun for the "Germ," he also completed the ballad of "Jan Van Hunks," and wrote a couple of sonnets for his drawing called the "Question."

Most of the critics who have written on Rossetti deplore the fact that he did not learn to paint, but to artists one of the greatest charms of his pictures (especially the early ones) is the un-expectedness of their composition. We owe that charm in a great measure to the fact that happily he had not been spoiled by the sophisticated teaching of Academic Schools, but had kept the bloom of his poetical inspiration. We must thank the instinct of the young man, which made him avoid a teaching which is bound to be fatal to both realism and romanticism. It may be that he himself deplored the lack of training at certain moments of discouragement in his life, but the kind of training available at the time of his début would not have added much to his achievement. He managed to say what he had to say, and in many cases to say it well. He saved himself the loss of time necessary to forget certain of the artistic préjugés then in vogue, they would have been very much in his way, even if he had quite succeeded in getting rid of them. The rather amateurish side to Rossetti's art is vastly compensated for by the precious qualities he has been able to preserve.

It is unfortunate that, through his refusal to exhibit, the public has been acquainted first with his later work, which shows the decline of his faculties caused by his ill health. Neither the fresh creations of his early work nor the gorgeous pieces of his middle period are as well known as they deserve to be.

As a young man Rossetti possessed an extraordinary influence over the members of the group round him. Later when his work became less sincere his influence declined and what promised to be at the beginning a great renaissance of the English School has ended with him. Such a disaster is certain to befall the school or the artists who do not refresh themselves continually by the "communion" with nature. Ruskin says in his Pre-Raphaelitism: "If they adhere to their principles, and paint nature as it is around them, with the help of modern science, with the earnestness of the men of the thirteenth and fourteenth centuries, they will, as I said, found a new and noble school in England. If their sympathies with the early artists lead them into mediævalism or Romanism, they will of course come to nothing." These words were prophetic.

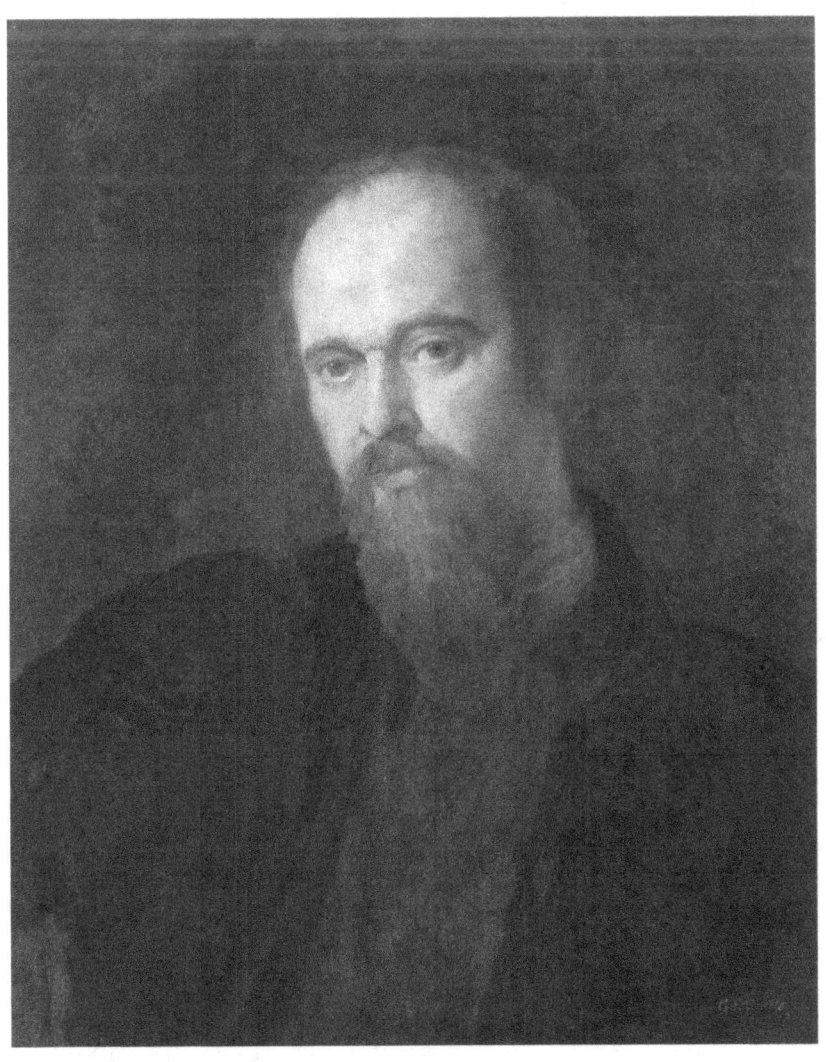

George Frederic Watts, Portrait of Dante Gabriel Rossetti

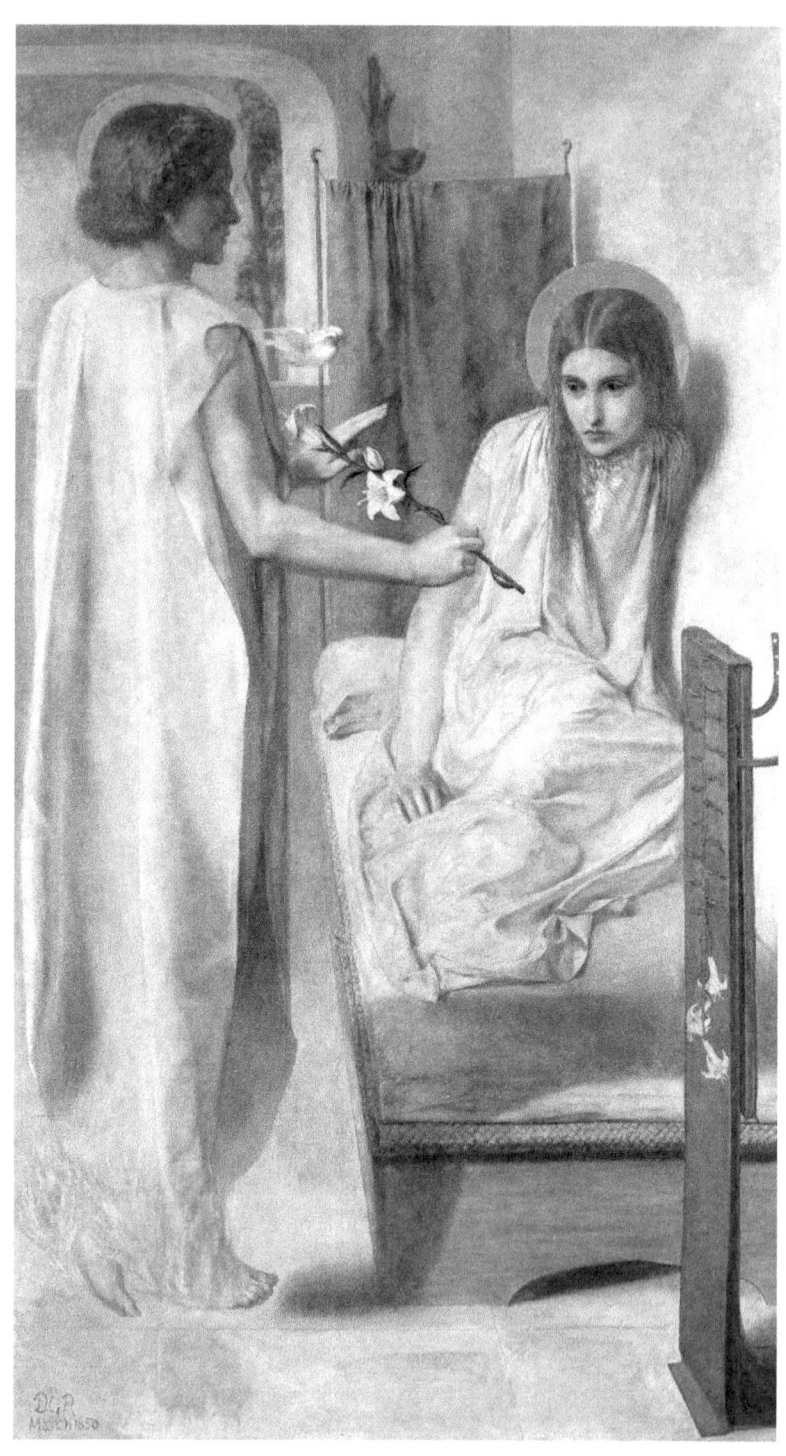

Dante Gabriel Rossetti, Ecce Ancilla Domini, 1850, Tate Britain

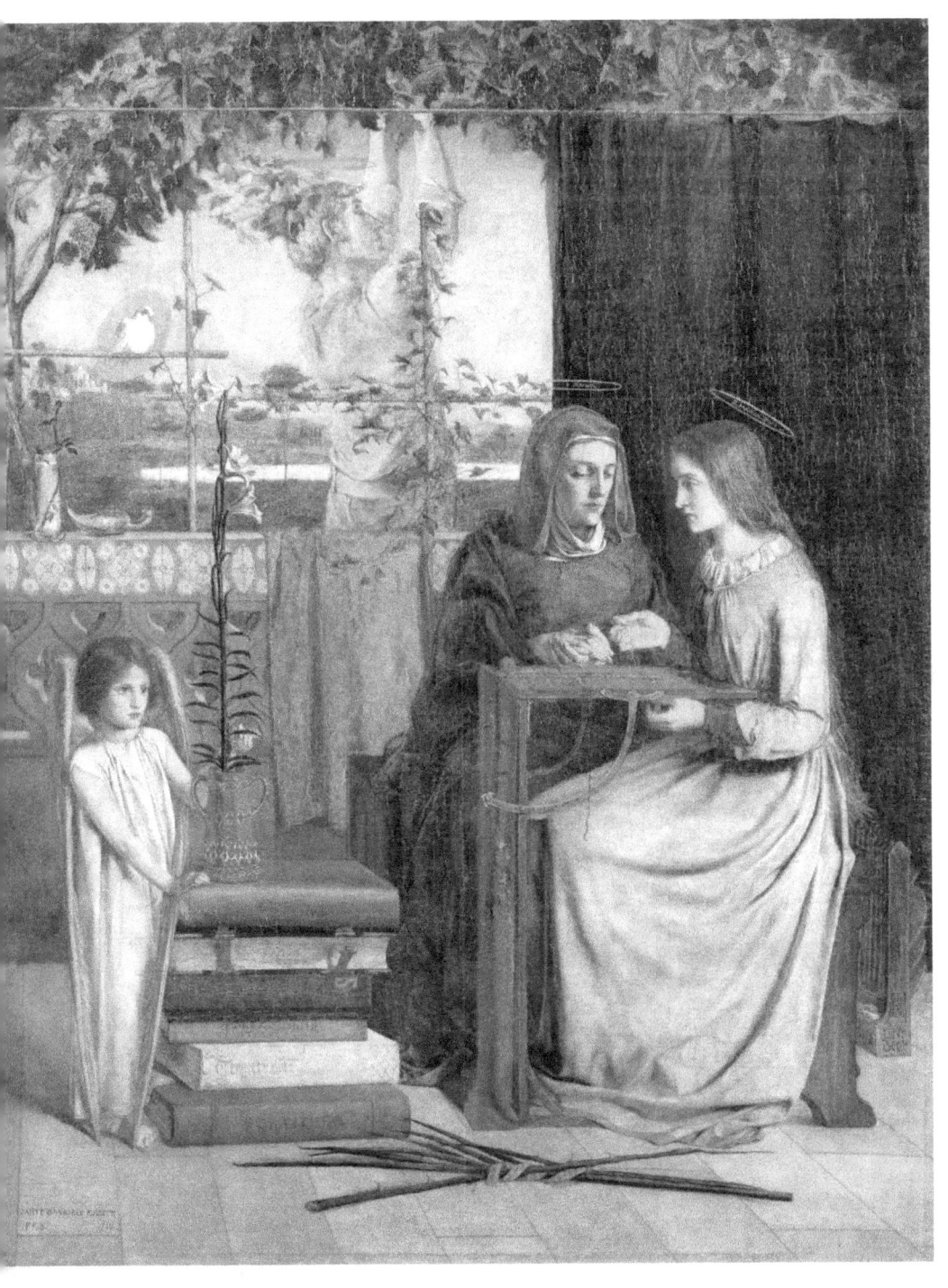

Dante Gabriel Rossetti, The Girlhood of Mary Virgin, Tate Britain

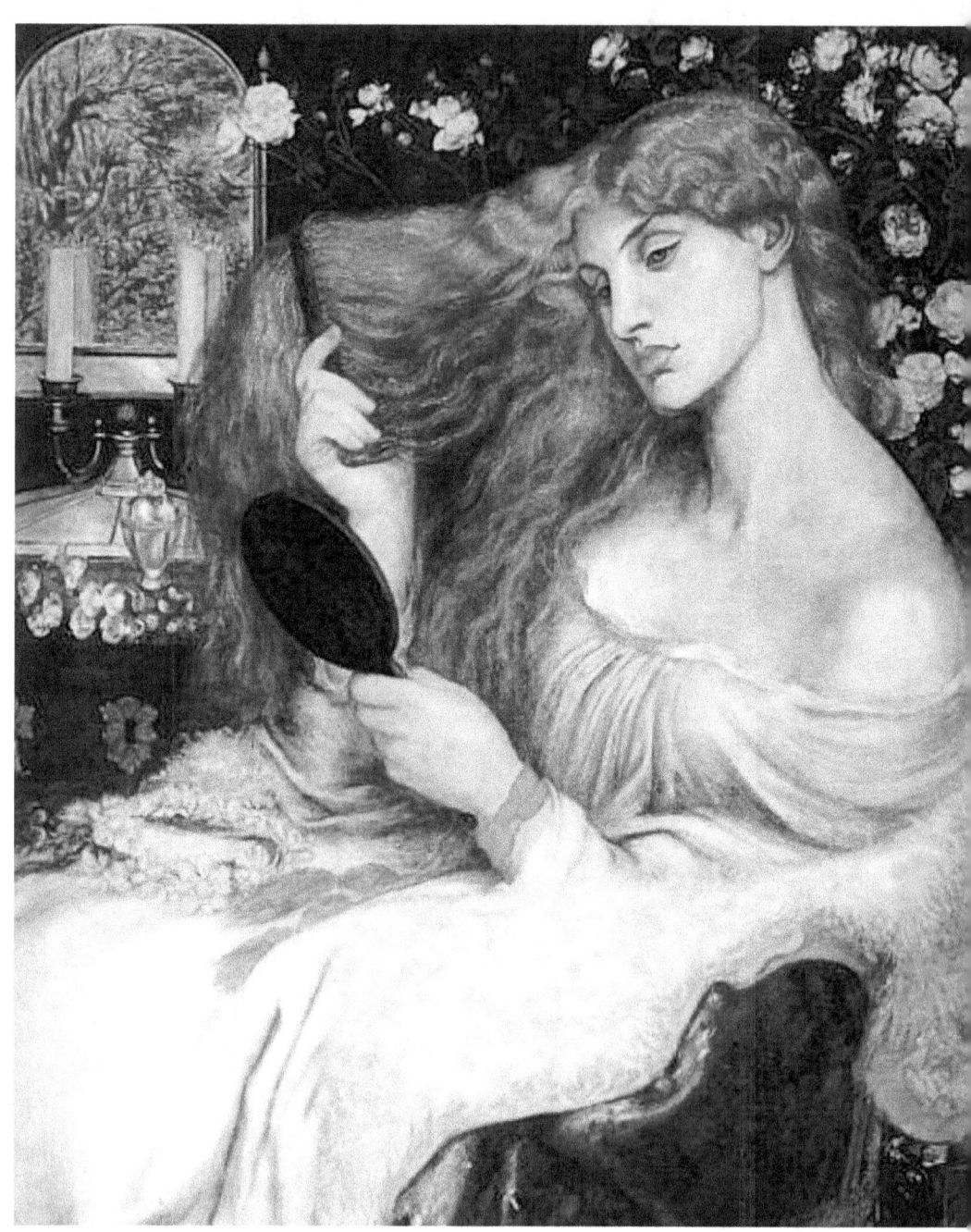

Dante Gabriel Rossetti, Lady Lilith, 1866-68, Delaware Art Museum

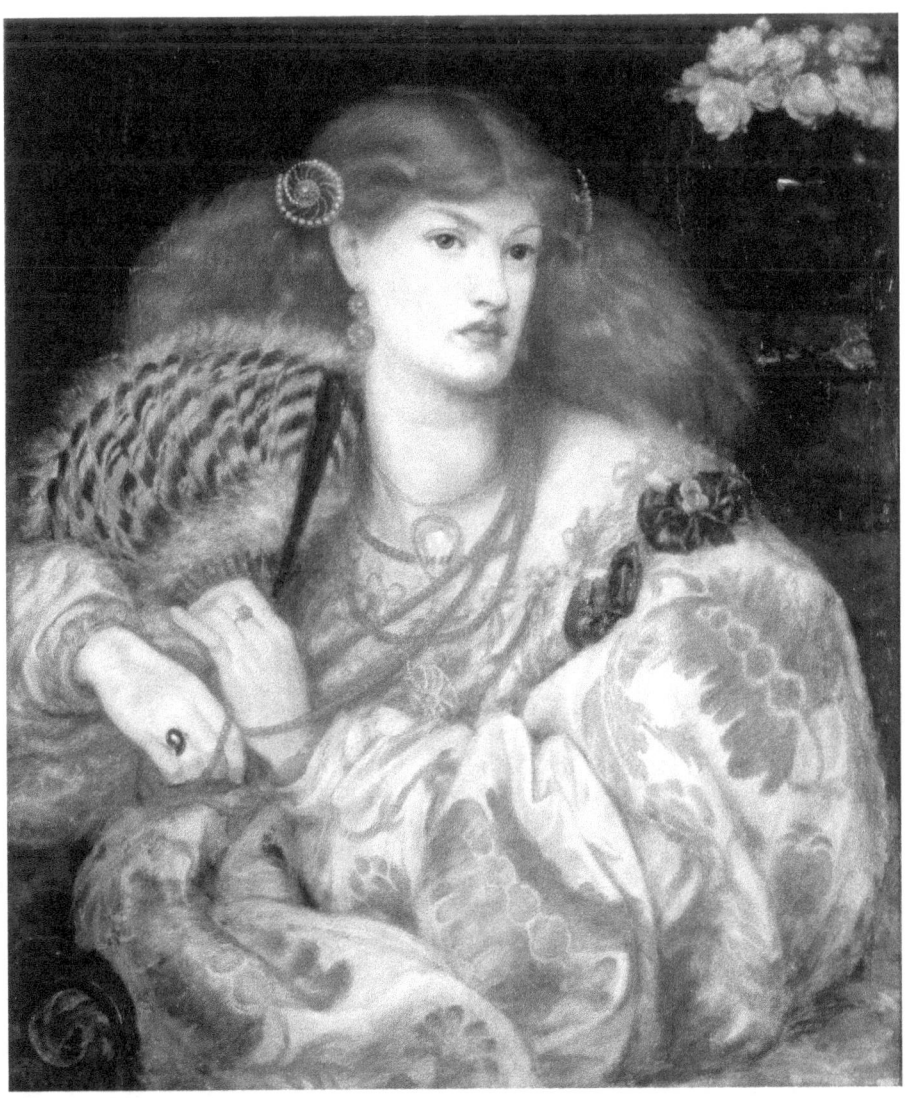

Dante Gabriel Rossetti, Monna Vanna, 1866, Tate Britain

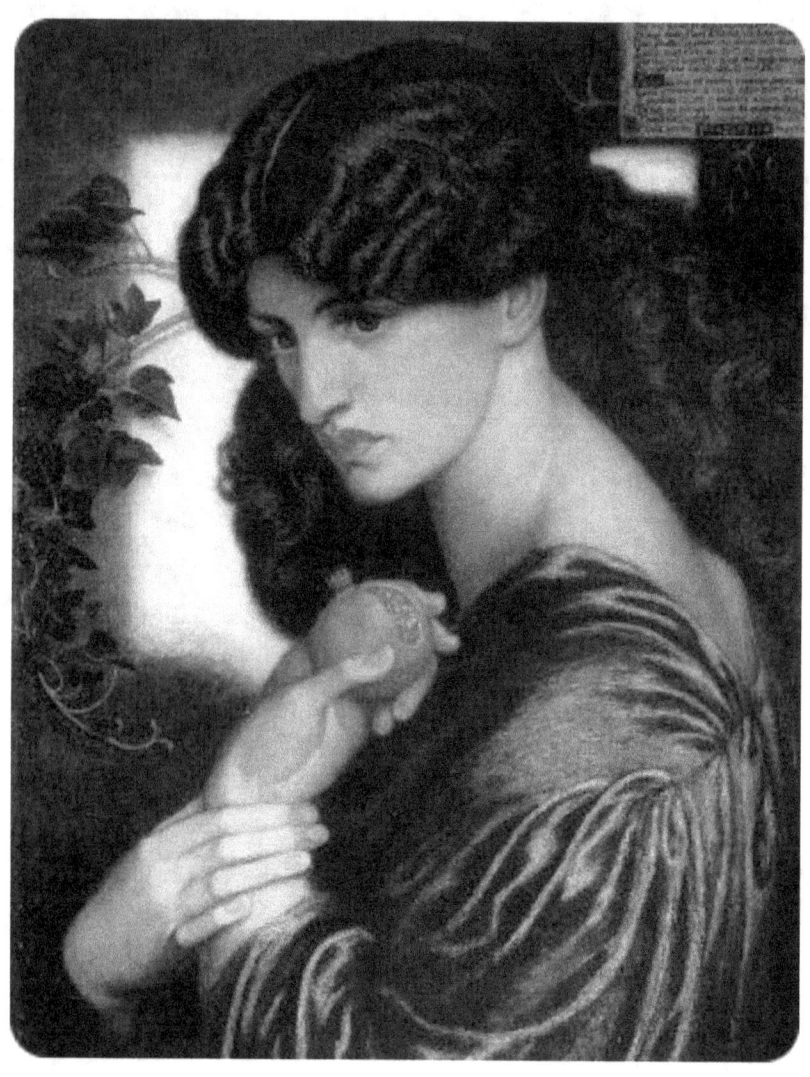

Dante Gabriel Rossetti, Prosperine, 1874, Tate Britain

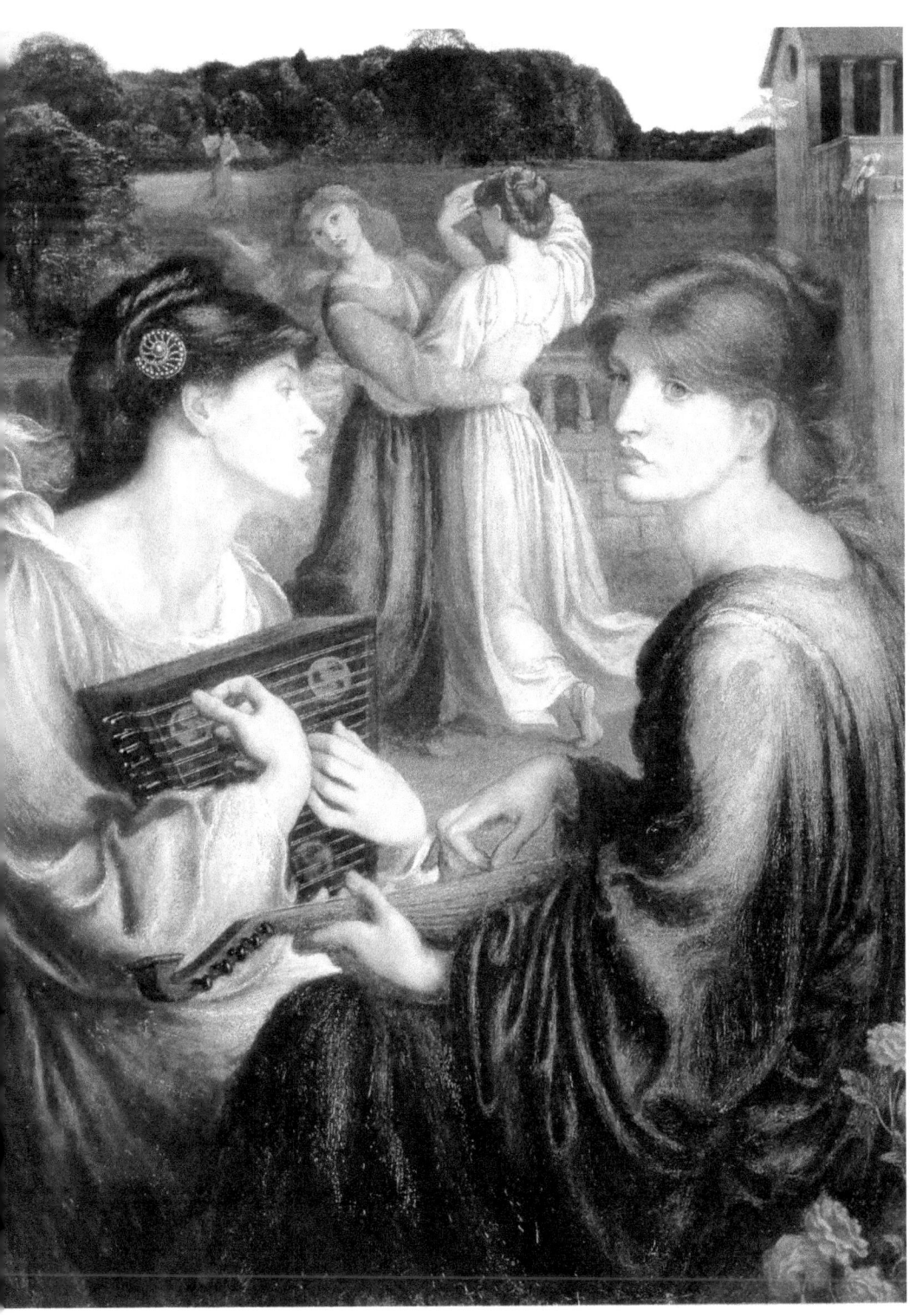

Dante Gabriel Rossetti, The Bower Meadow, 1872, Manchester

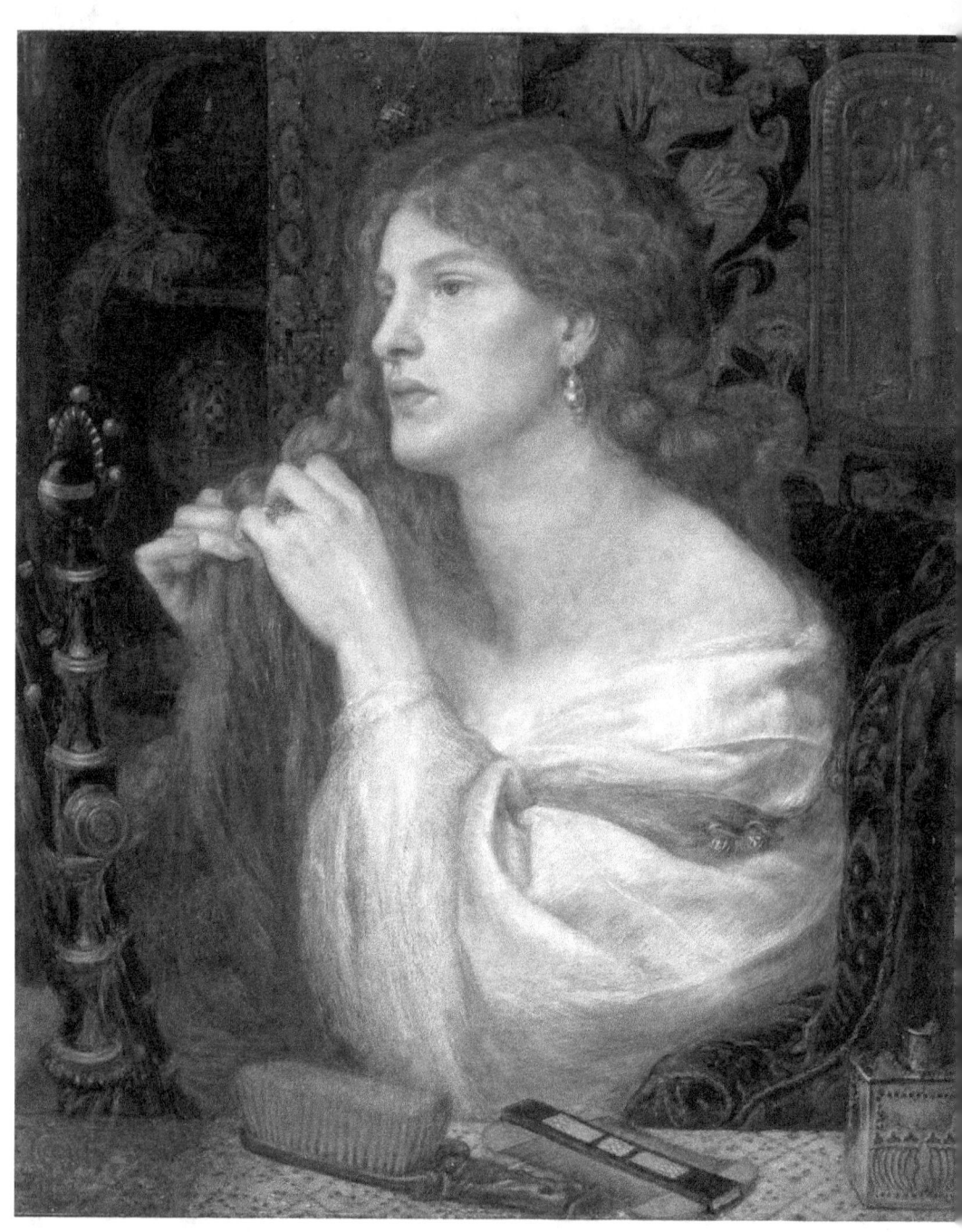

Dante Gabriel Rossetti, Aurelia (Fazio's Mistress), 1863/ 73, Tate Britain

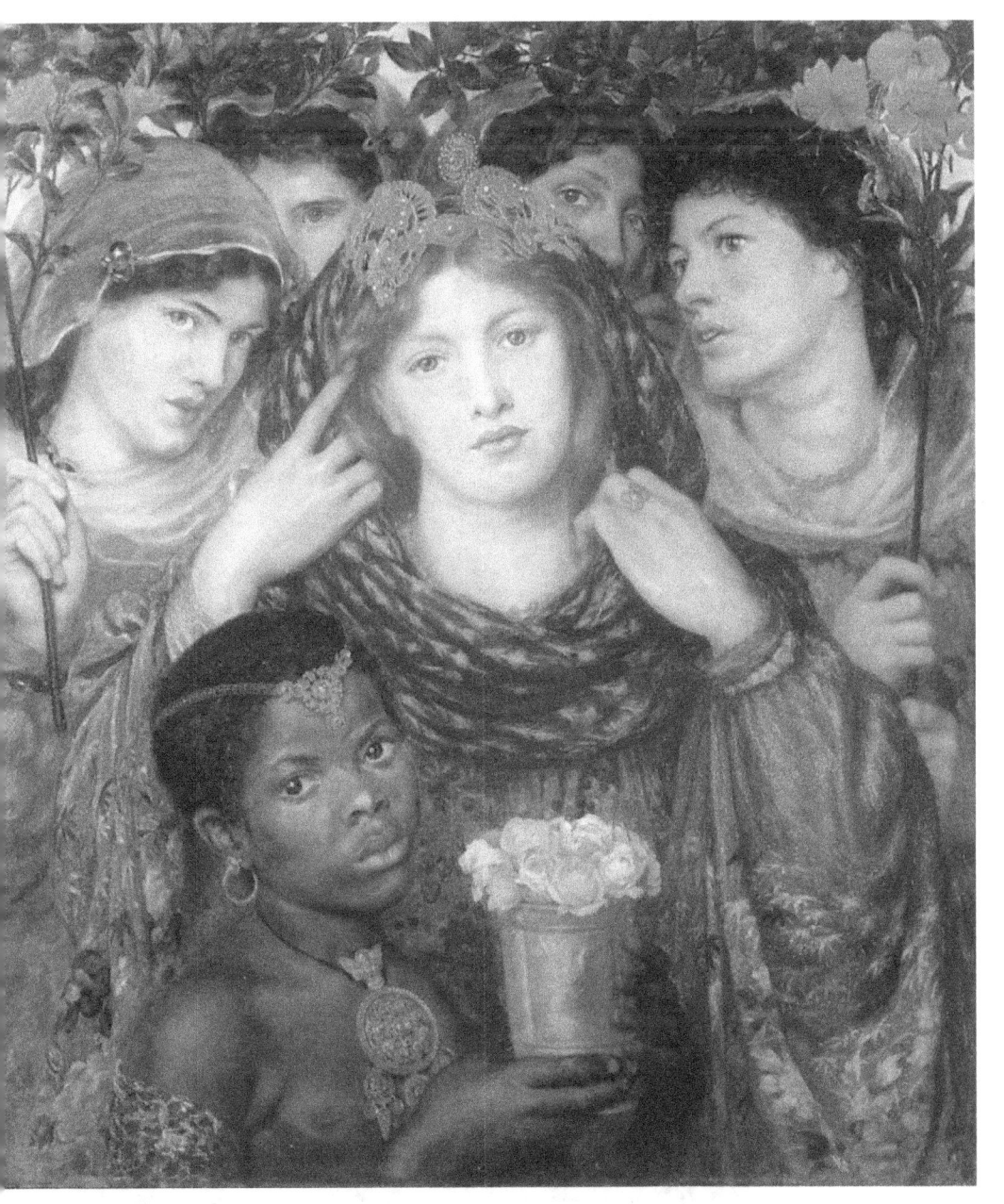

Dante Gabriel Rossetti, Die Geliebte, 1866, Tate Britain

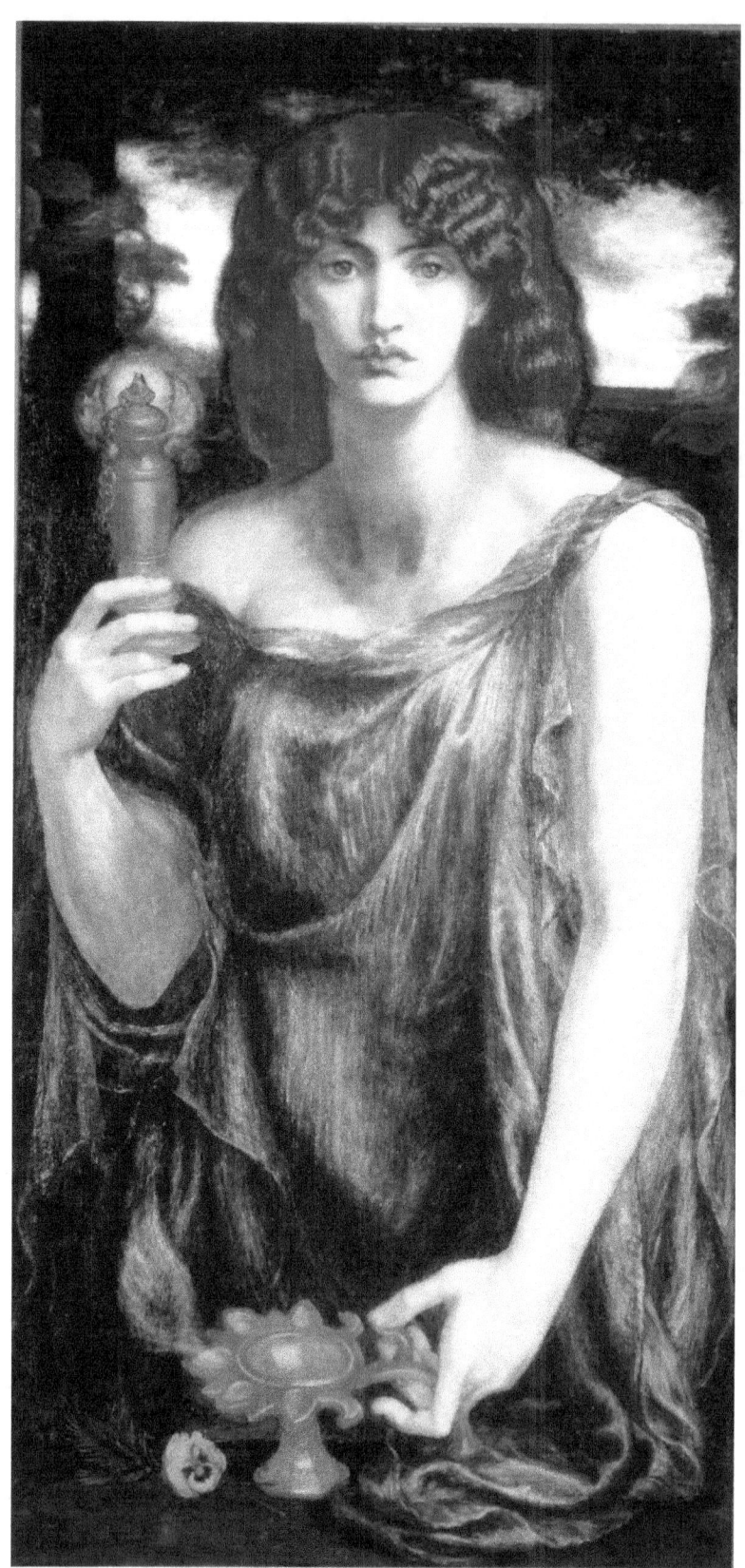

Dante Gabriel
Rossetti,
Mnemosyne,
Delaware

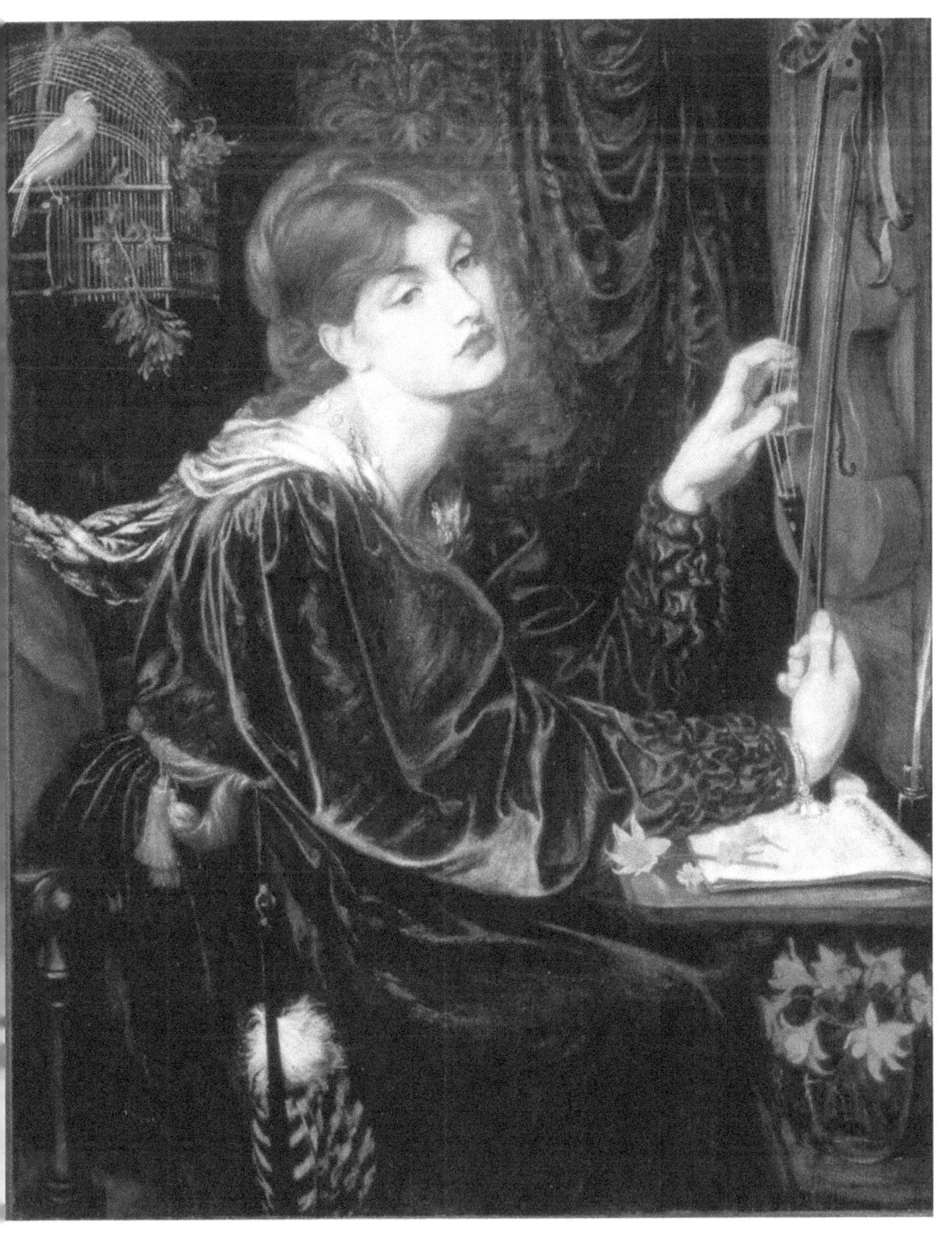

Dante Gabriel Rossetti, Veronica Veronese, 1872, Delaware

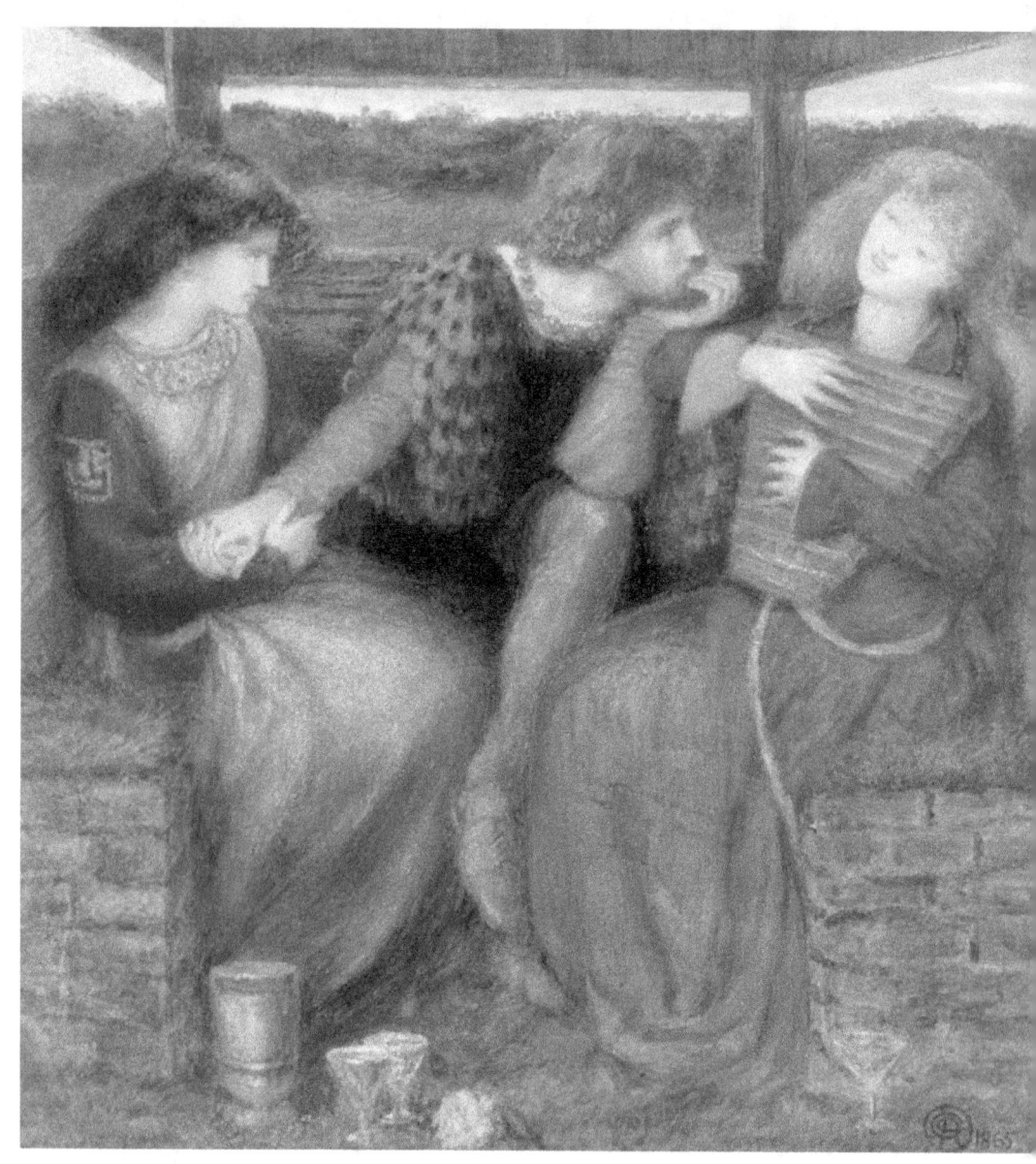

Dante Gabriel Rossetti, The Merciless Lady, 1865, private collection

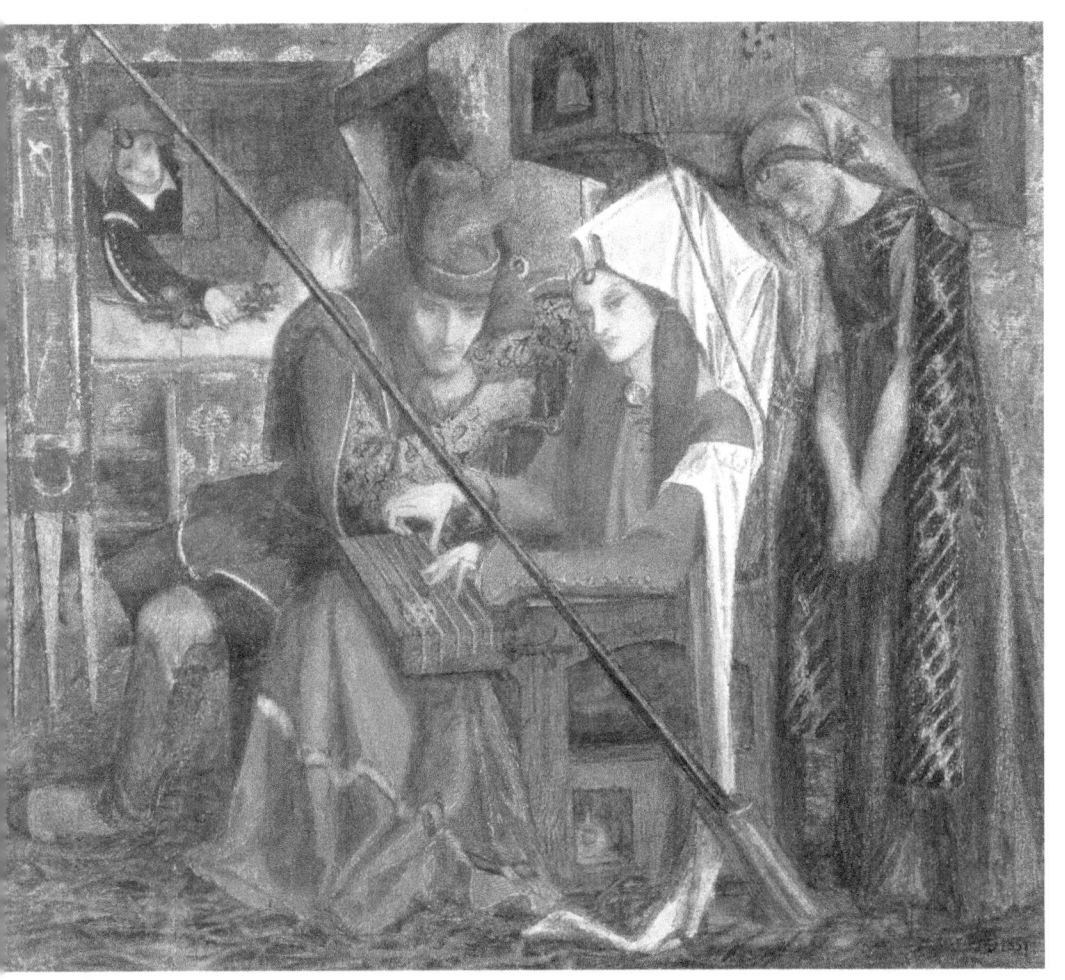

Dante Gabriel Rossetti, The Tune of Seven Towers, 1857, Tate Britain

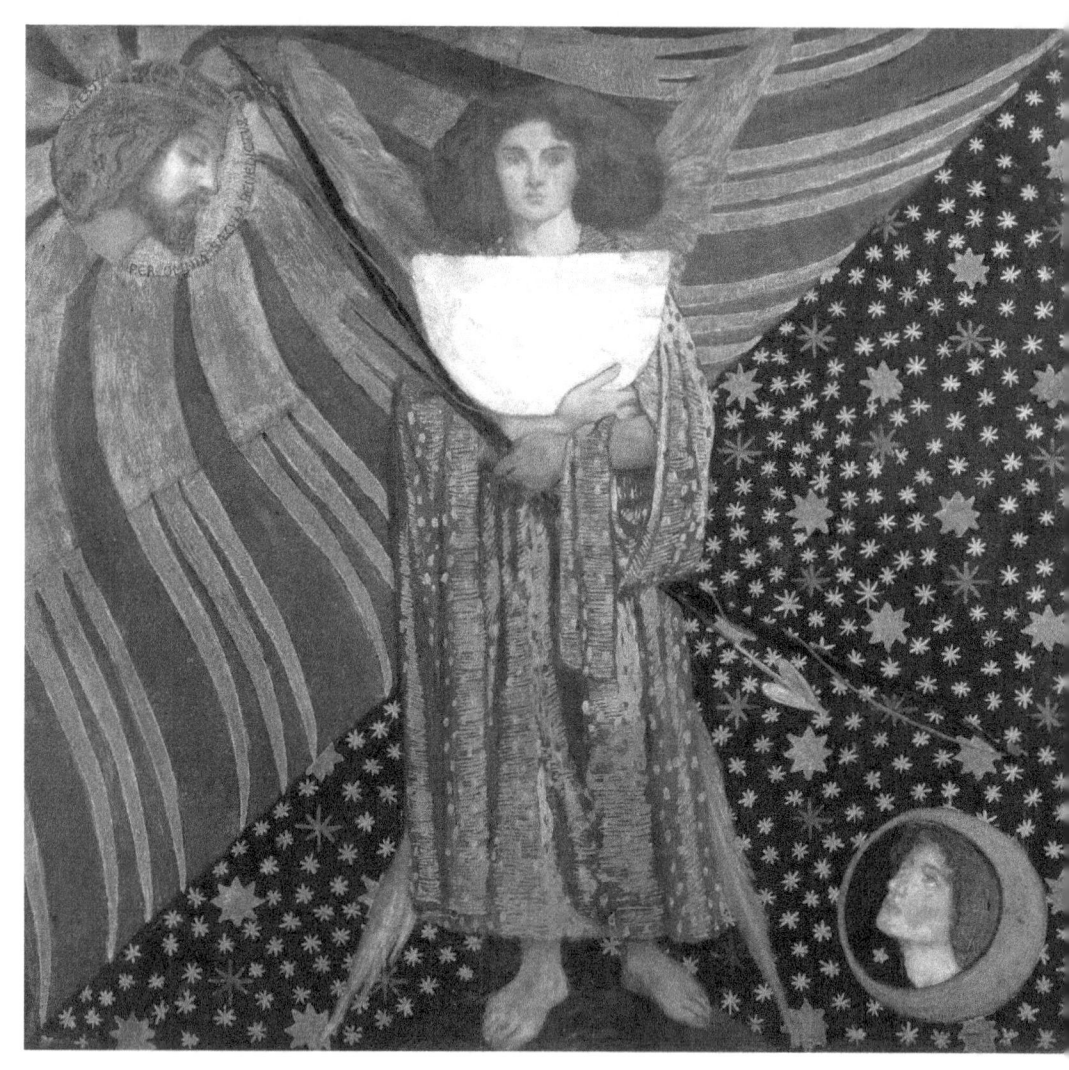

Dante Gabriel Rossetti, Dantis Amor, Tate Britain

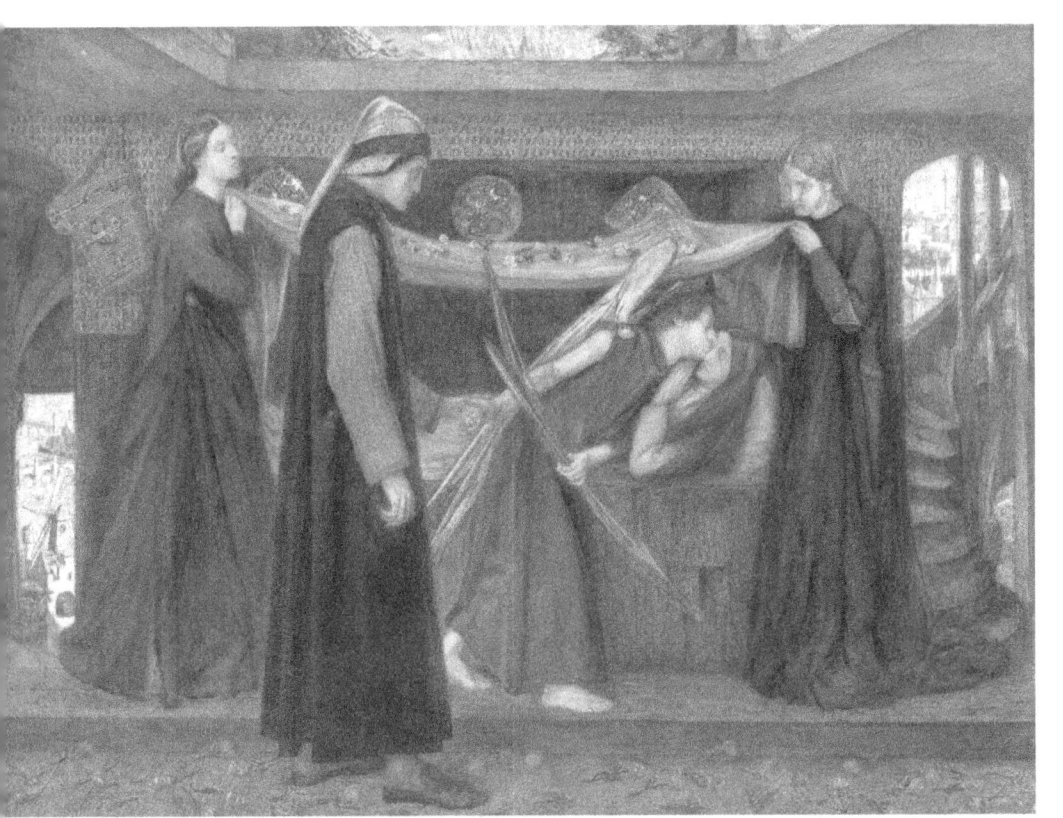

Dante Gabriel Rossetti, Dante's Dream, 1856, watercolour version, Tate Britain

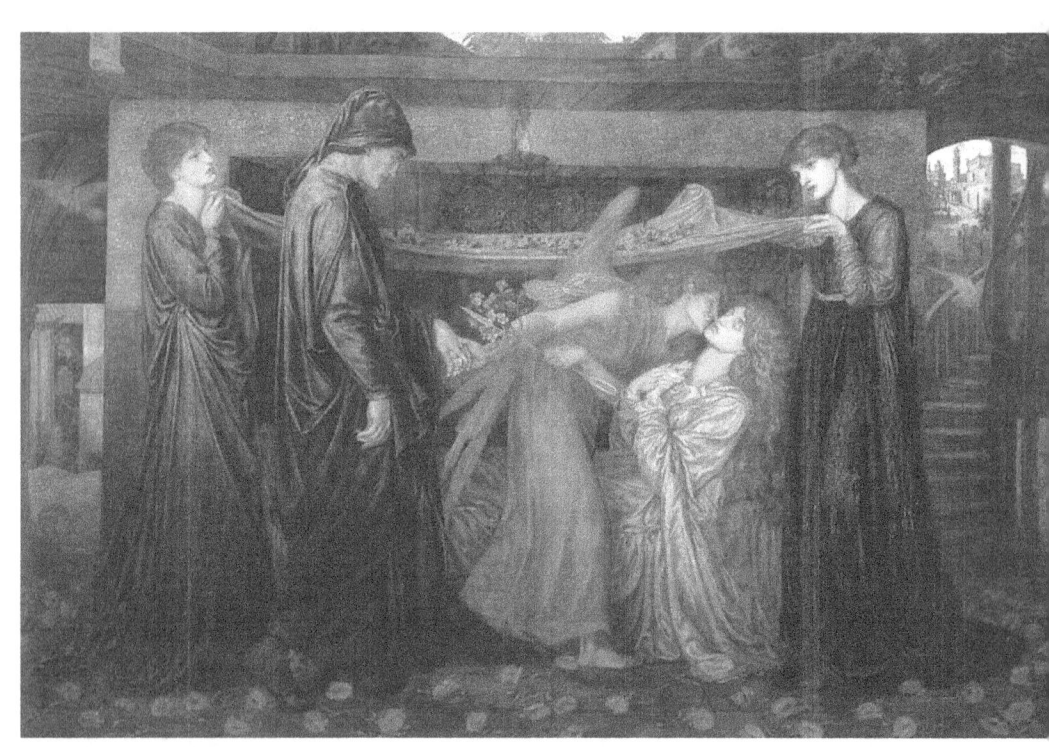

Dante Gabriel Rossetti, Dante's Dream, 1871,
Walker Art Gallery

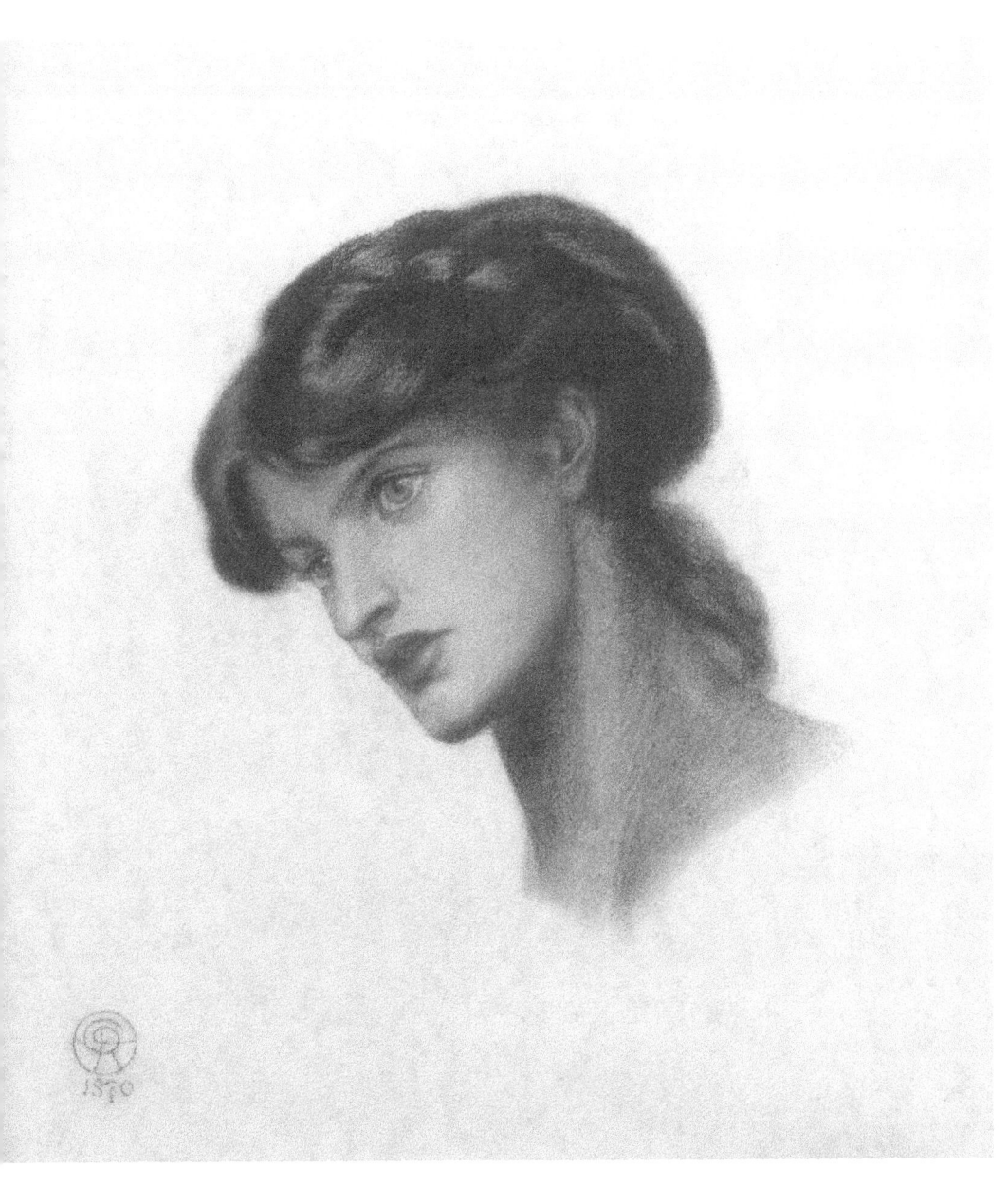

Dante Gabriel Rossetti, Study For 'Dante's Dream', Mrs. Stillman, 1870

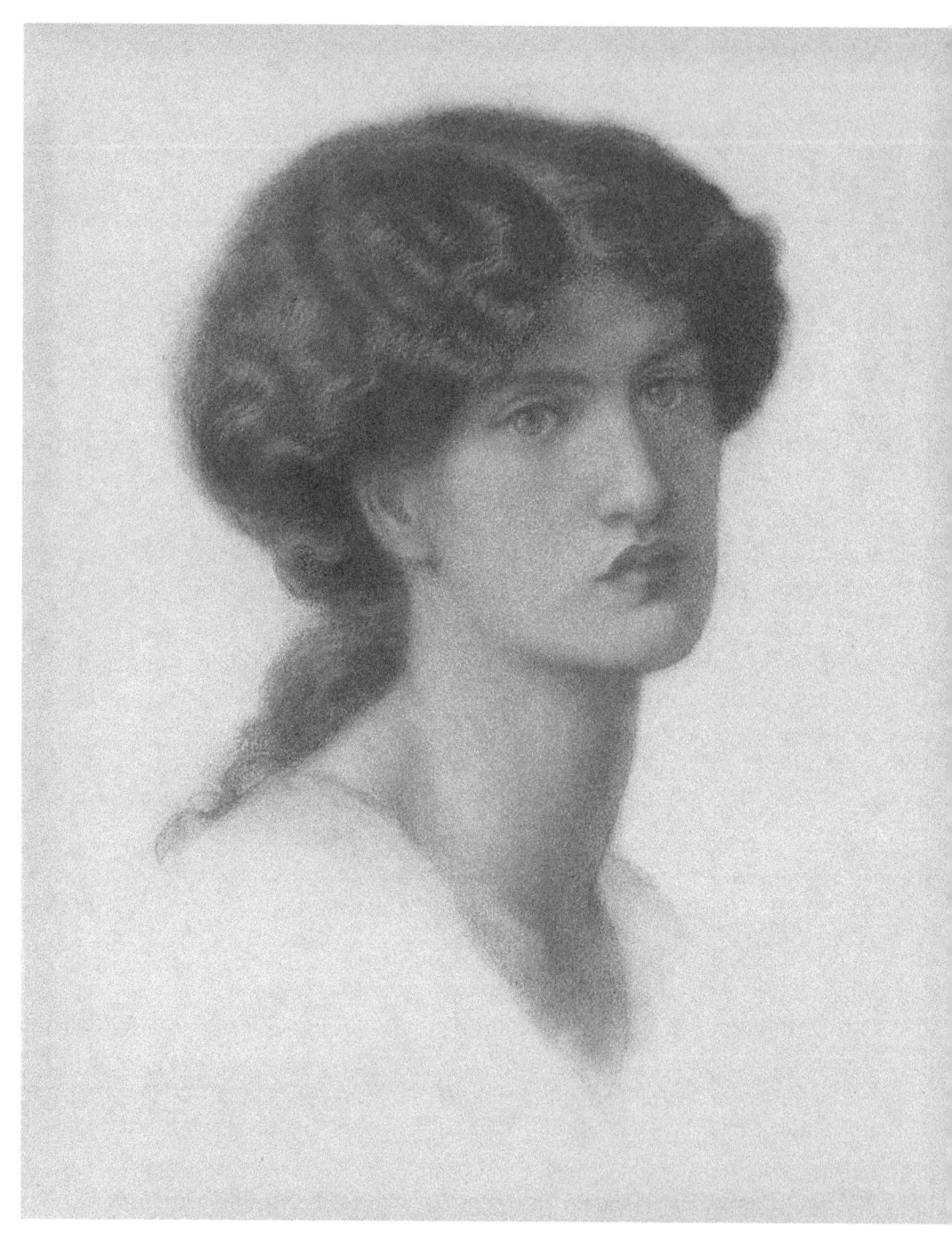

Dante Gabriel Rossetti, Portrait of Jane Morris, c. 1870

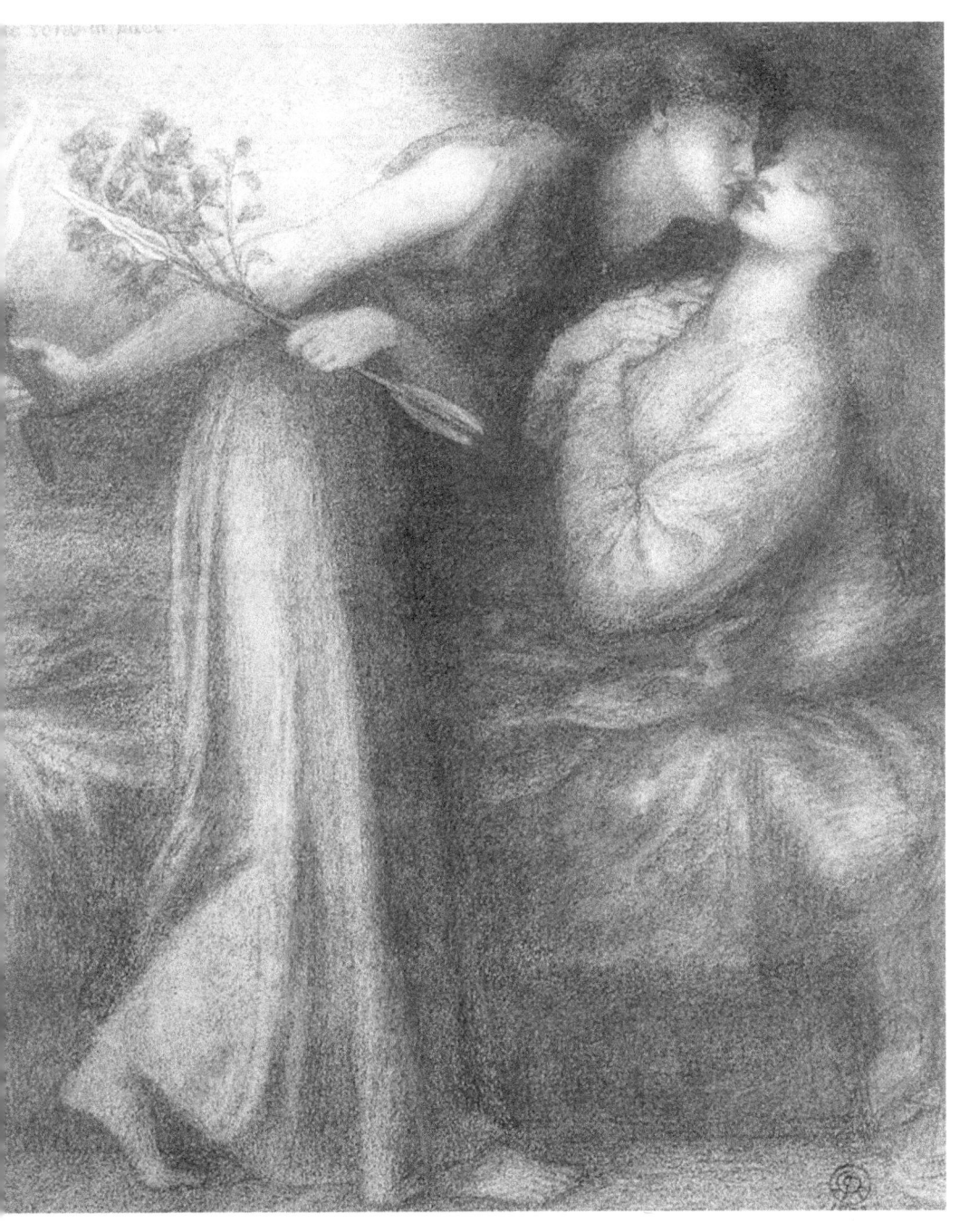

Dante Gabriel Rossetti, Io Sono In Pace, 1875, private collection

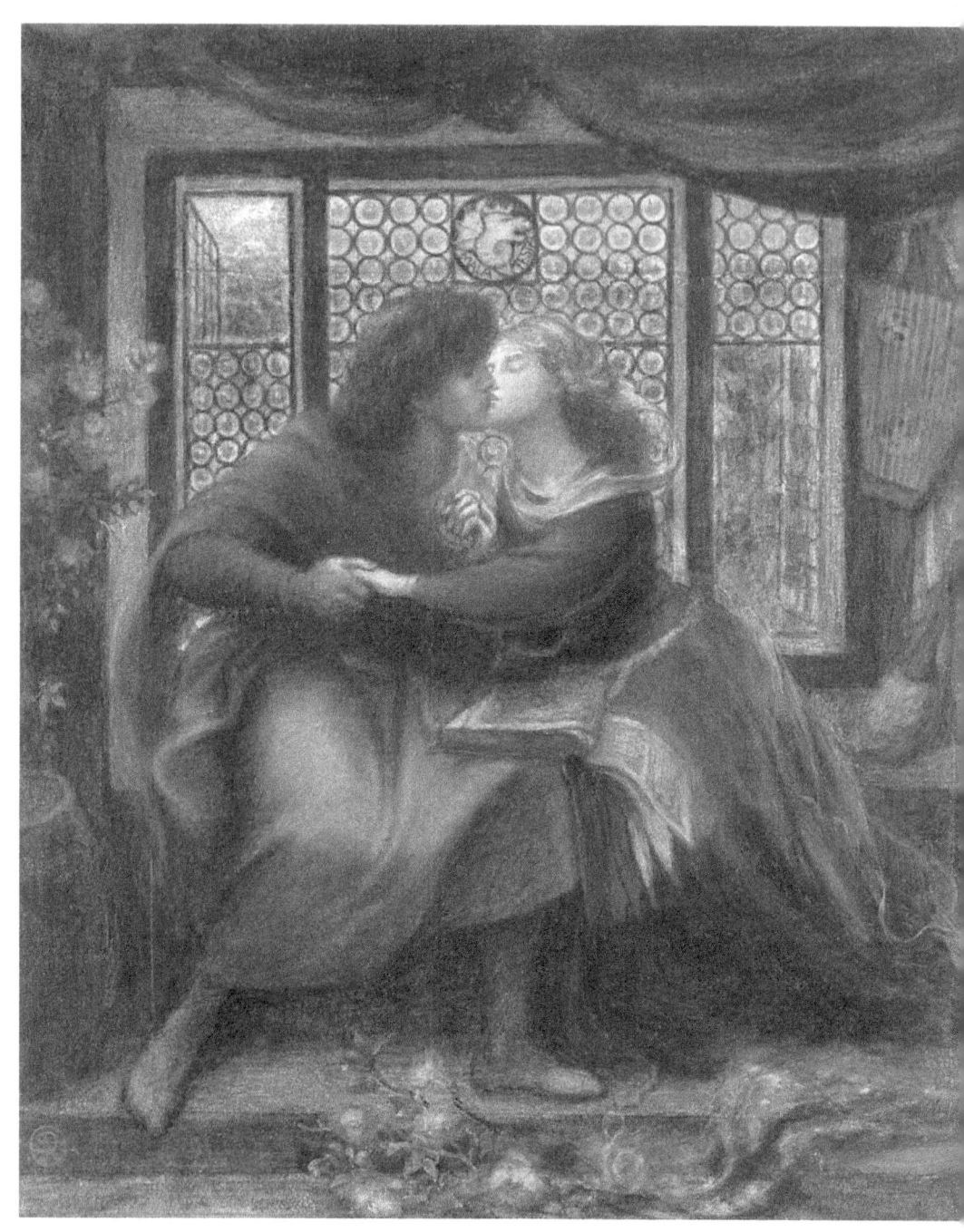

Dante Gabriel Rossetti, Paolo and Francesca da Rimini
1867, Melbourne

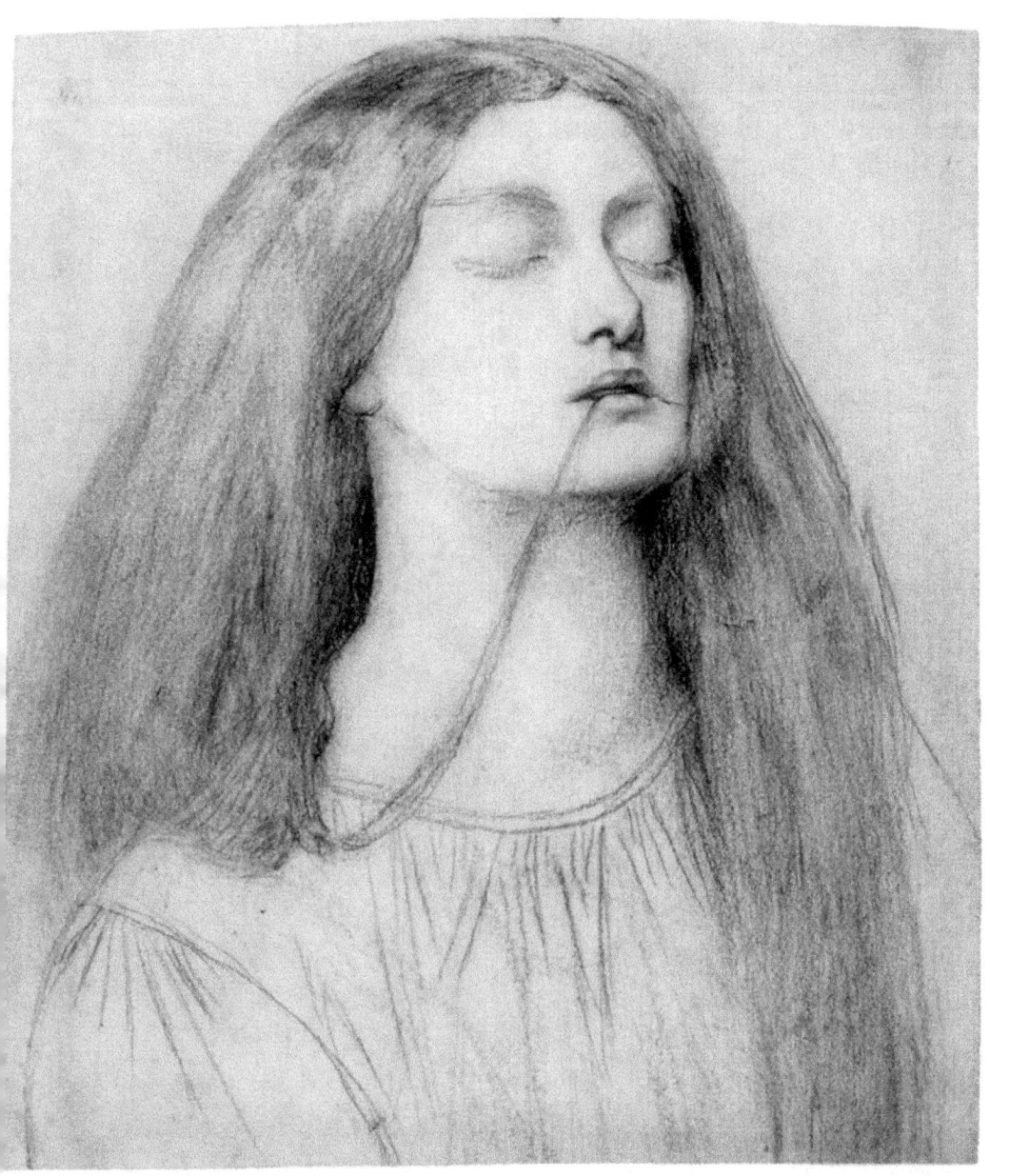

Dante Gabriel Rossetti, Elizabeth Siddal (Study For Delia), 1862, Cambridge

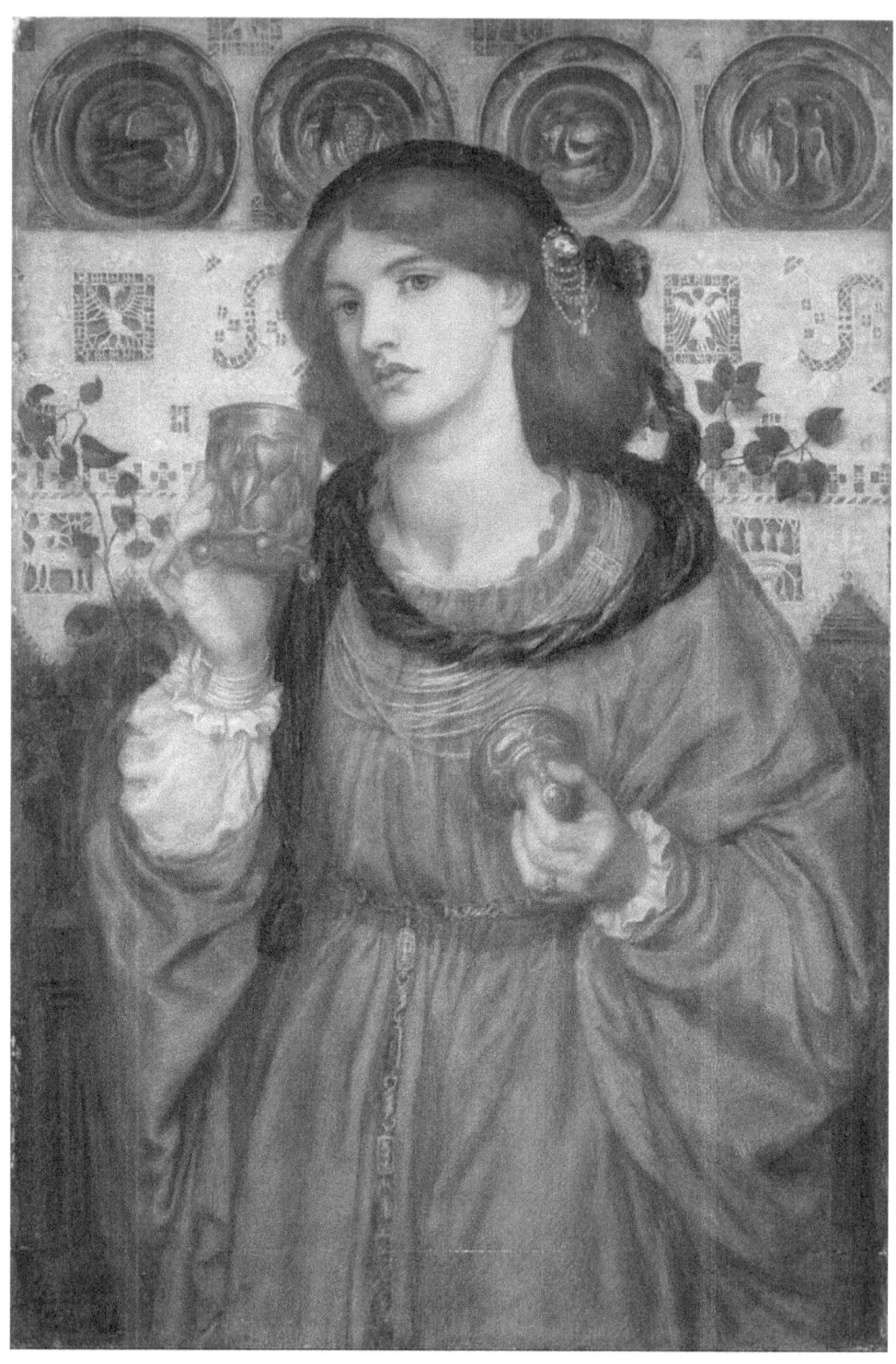

Dante Gabriel Rossetti, The Loving Cup, 1867, Tokyo

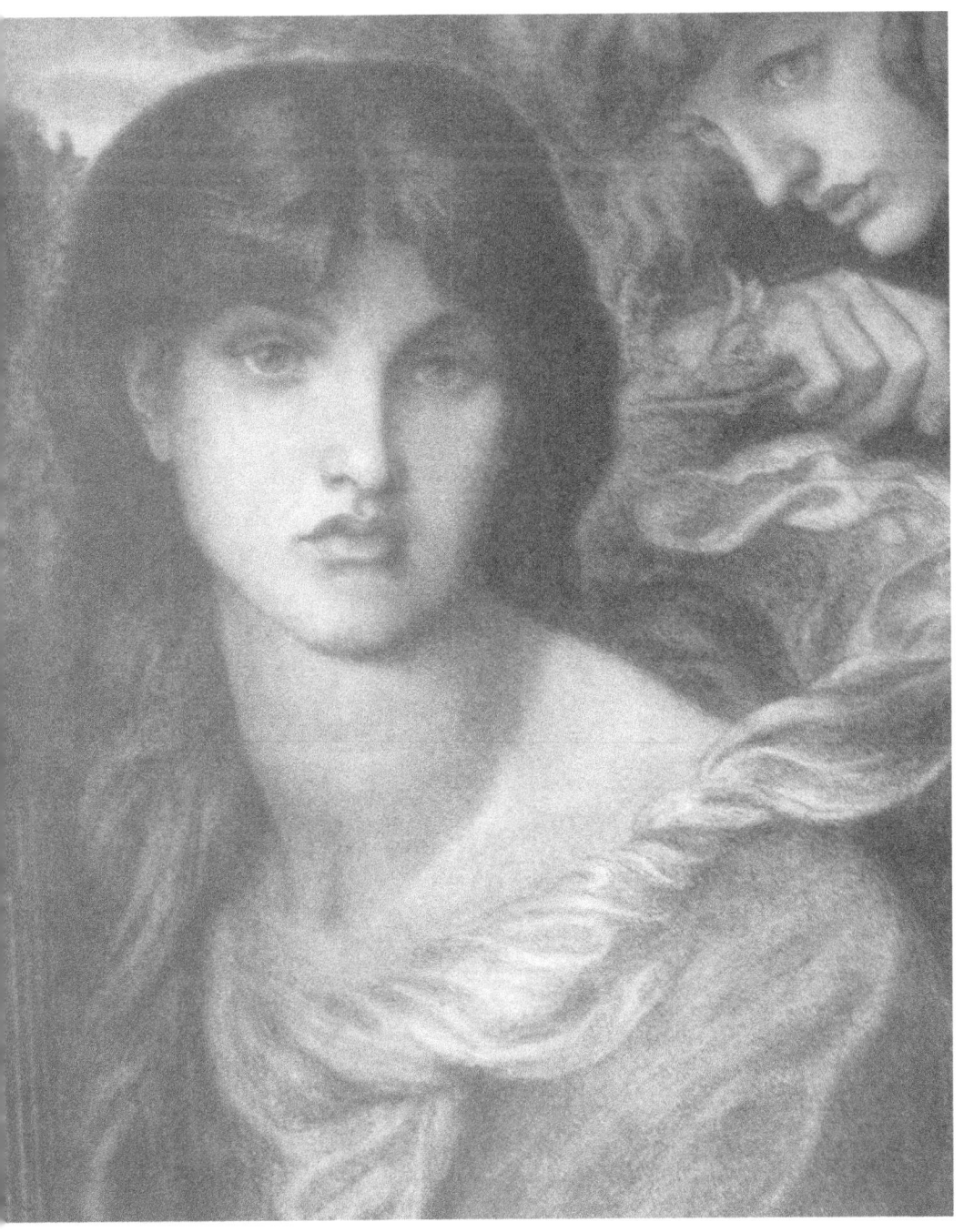

Dante Gabriel Rossetti, Ghirlandata, 1873, detail

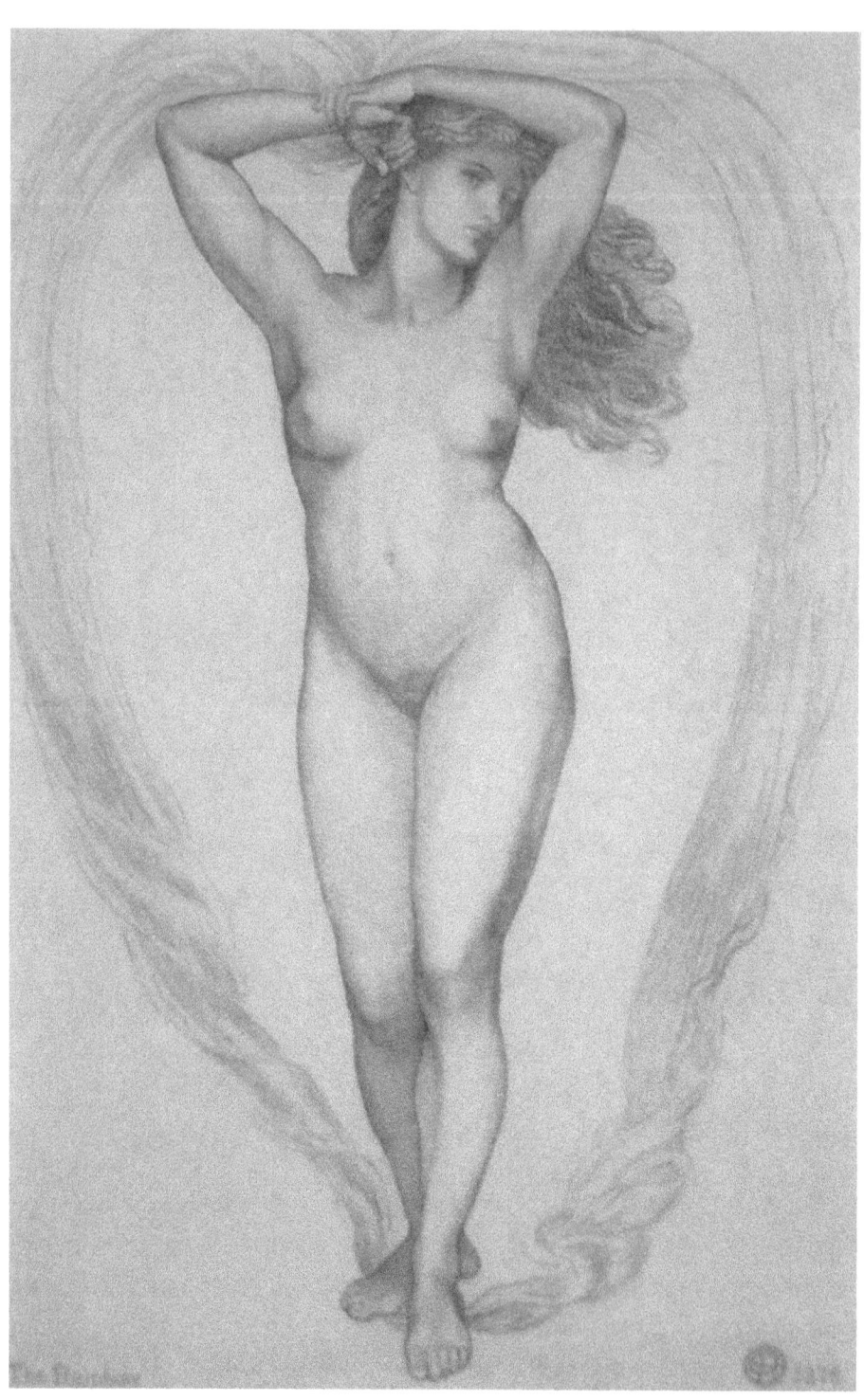

Dante Gabriel Rossetti, Spirit of the Rainbow, 1876

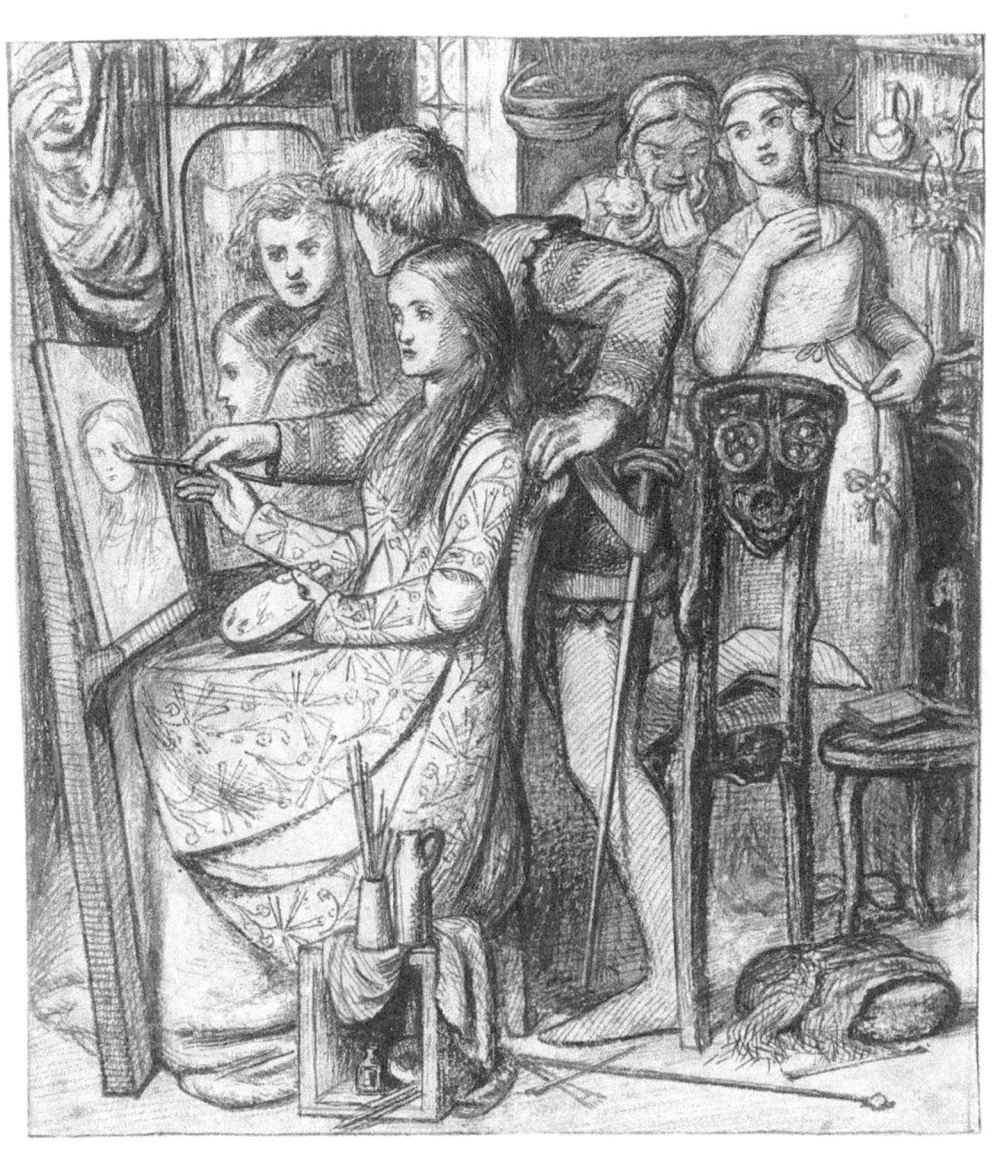

Dante Gabriel Rossetti, Love's Mirror or a Parable of Love ,
1850-52, Birmingham

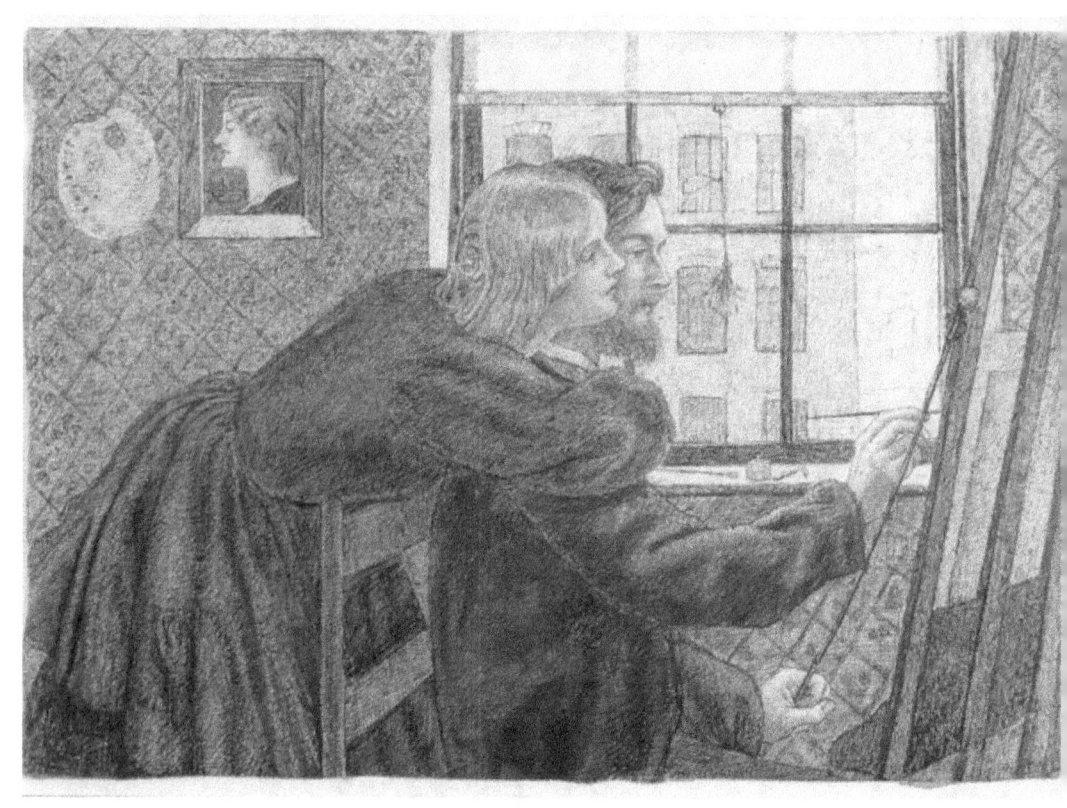

Dante Gabriel Rossetti, Fanny Cornforth and George Price Boyce, 1858

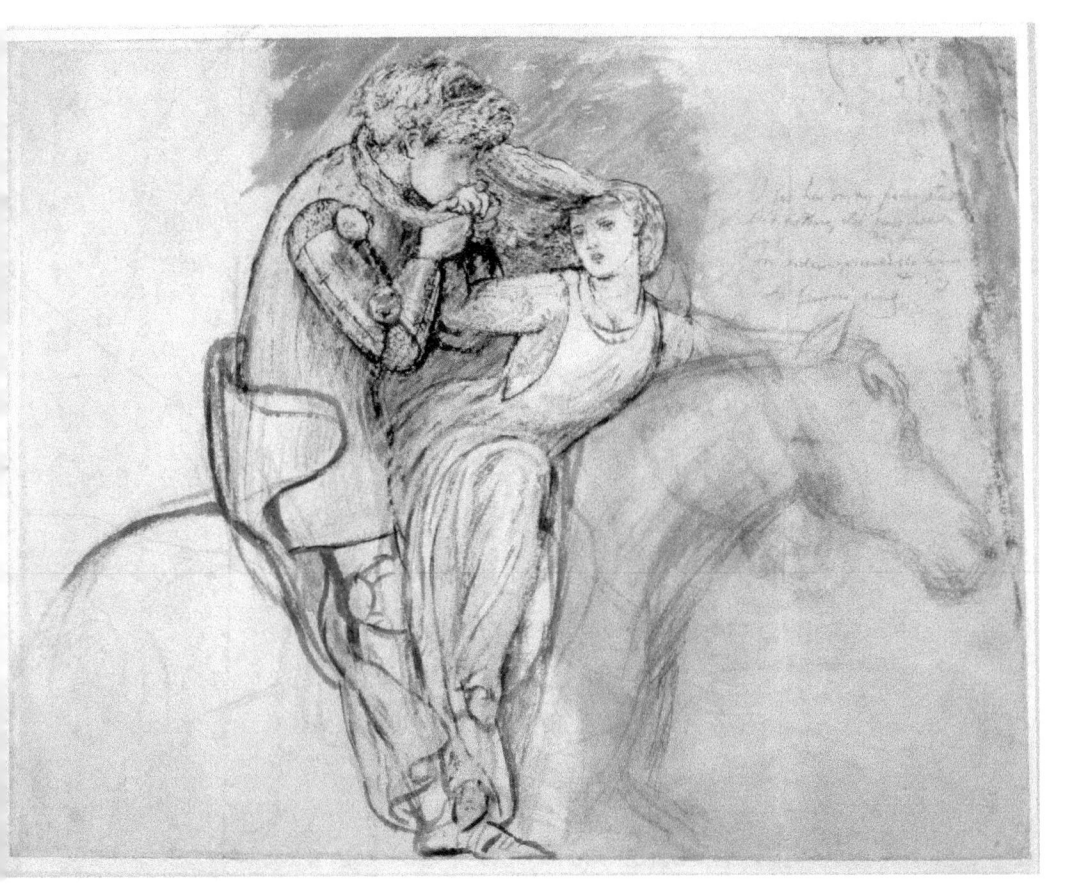

Dante Gabriel Rossetti, La Belle Dame Sans Merci, 1855

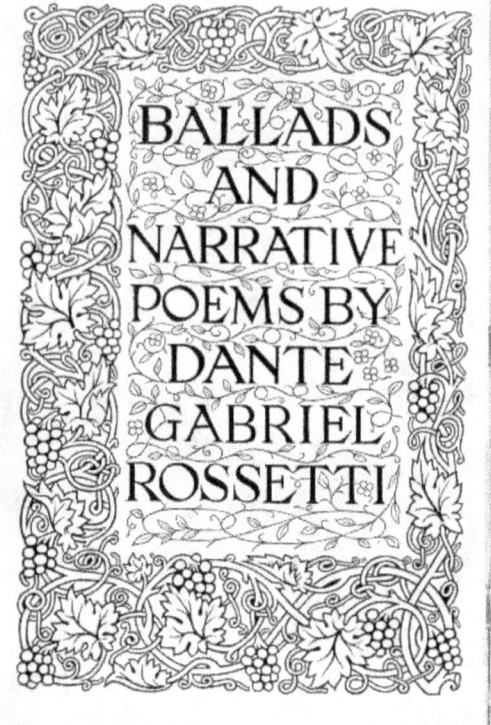

BALLADS
AND
NARRATIVE
POEMS BY
DANTE
GABRIEL
ROSSETTI

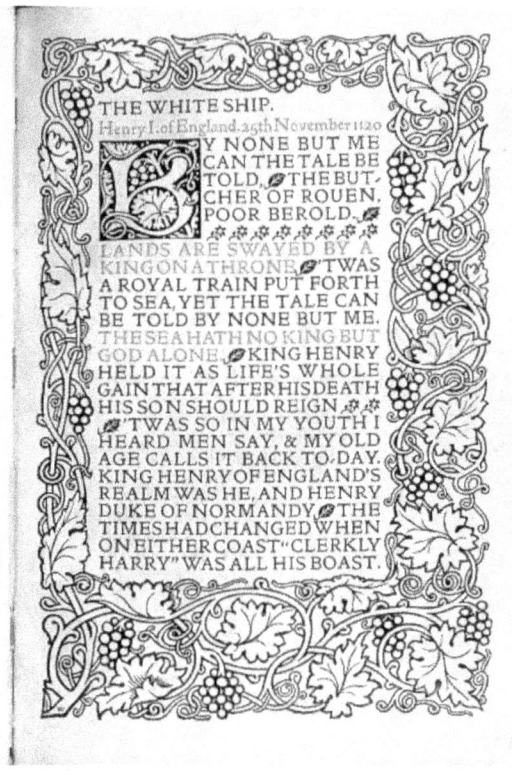

THE WHITE SHIP.
Henry I. of England. 25th November 1120

BY NONE BUT ME CAN THE TALE BE TOLD, THE BUT-CHER OF ROUEN, POOR BEROLD. LANDS ARE SWAYED BY A KING ON A THRONE. 'TWAS A ROYAL TRAIN PUT FORTH TO SEA, YET THE TALE CAN BE TOLD BY NONE BUT ME. THE SEA HATH NO KING BUT GOD ALONE. KING HENRY HELD IT AS LIFE'S WHOLE GAIN THAT AFTER HIS DEATH HIS SON SHOULD REIGN. 'TWAS SO IN MY YOUTH I HEARD MEN SAY, & MY OLD AGE CALLS IT BACK TO-DAY. KING HENRY OF ENGLAND'S REALM WAS HE, AND HENRY DUKE OF NORMANDY. THE TIMES HAD CHANGED WHEN ON EITHER COAST "CLERKLY HARRY" WAS ALL HIS BOAST.

Dante Gabriel Rossetti, title page

NOTES ON THE WORKS

PLATE I. – THE DAYDREAM

From the oil painting (61? in. by 35 in.) painted in 1880 and first exhibited in the Royal Academy in 1883.

This picture was painted from Mrs. William Morris and was left to South Kensington by Constantine Ionidès, Esq.

PLATE II. – ECCE ANCILLA DOMINI

From the oil painting (28? in. by 17 in.) painted in 1850 and is now in the Tate Gallery

This picture was first exhibited in 1850 at the "Free Exhibition" in Portland Place. It was very slightly retouched in 1873 for the then owner, Mr. Graham. It is rightly considered the most typical of Rossetti's "Pre-Raphaelite" period.

PLATE III. – DANTE DRAWING THE ANGEL

From the water-colour (16? in. by 24 in.) painted in 1853 and first exhibited in the Pre-Raphaelite Exhibition at Russell Place in 1857. It is now in the Taylorian Museum at Oxford

The subject of this water-colour is taken from the following passage in the Vita Nuova:

"On that day which fulfilled the year since my lady had been made of the citizens of eternal life, remembering me of her as I sat alone, I betook myself to draw the resemblance of an angel upon certain tablets. And while I did thus, chancing to turn my head I perceived that some were standing beside me, to whom I should have given courteous welcome, and that they were observing what I did: also I learned afterwards that they had been there awhile before I perceived them. Perceiving whom, I arose for salutation and said: 'Another was with me.'"

The same incident has been commemorated by Robert Browning in his "One Word More."

PLATE IV. – BEATA BEATRIX

From the oil painting (34 in. by 27 in.) painted in 1863 for Lord Mount-Temple, now in the Tate Gallery

Though undoubtedly inspired by the death of his wife, the motive of this picture was ostensibly taken from the Vita Nuova. The Latin quotation inscribed on the frame, which was designed by Rossetti himself, is taken from the following passage:

"After this most gracious creature had gone out from among us, the whole city came to be as it were widowed and despoiled of all dignity. Then I, left mourning in this desolate city, wrote unto the principal persons thereof, in an epistle, concerning its condition; taking for my commencement those words of Jeremias: Quomodo sedet sola civitas! etc."

The date of the death of Beatrice is also inscribed on the frame.

PLATE V. – THE BOWER MEADOW

From the oil painting (32 in. by 25 in.) in the collection of the late Sir John Milburn, Bart., Acklington, Northumberland

Of this charming composition the landscape background was painted at Sevenoaks in 1850, and the figures were added and the whole finished in 1872.

PLATE VI. – THE BORGIA FAMILY

From the water-colour painted in 1873 and lately purchased by the South Kensington Museum

Rossetti first painted this subject in 1851 – a smaller size 9? by 10 in. It is one of the richest of his small compositions.

PLATE VII. – DANTE'S DREAM

From the oil painting (7 ft. 1 by 10 ft. 6?) now in the Walker Art Gallery, Liverpool

This picture which is considered by some to be Rossetti's most important work, illustrates the following passage in the Vita Nuova:

"Then my heart that was so full of love said unto me: 'Is it true that our lady lieth dead'; and it seemed to me that I went to look upon the body wherein that blessed and most noble spirit had had its abiding-place. And so strong was this idle imagining, that it made me behold my lady in death, whose head certain ladies seemed to be covering with a white veil."

This picture, painted in 1871, passed through several hands and was taken back by Rossetti from Mr. Valpy, on account of its large size in exchange for several smaller works. It was eventually bought by the Liverpool corporation.

Rossetti first treated this subject in a little water-colour painted for Miss Heaton in 1856.

PLATE VIII. – ASTARTE SYRIACA

From the oil painting (74 in. by 43 in.) now in the Corporation Art Gallery at Manchester

This picture was painted for Mr. Clarence Fry of the firm Elliot and Fry, in 1877 and was first exhibited at the Royal Academy in 1883.

On the following pages are some illustrations of contemporaries of Rosetti.

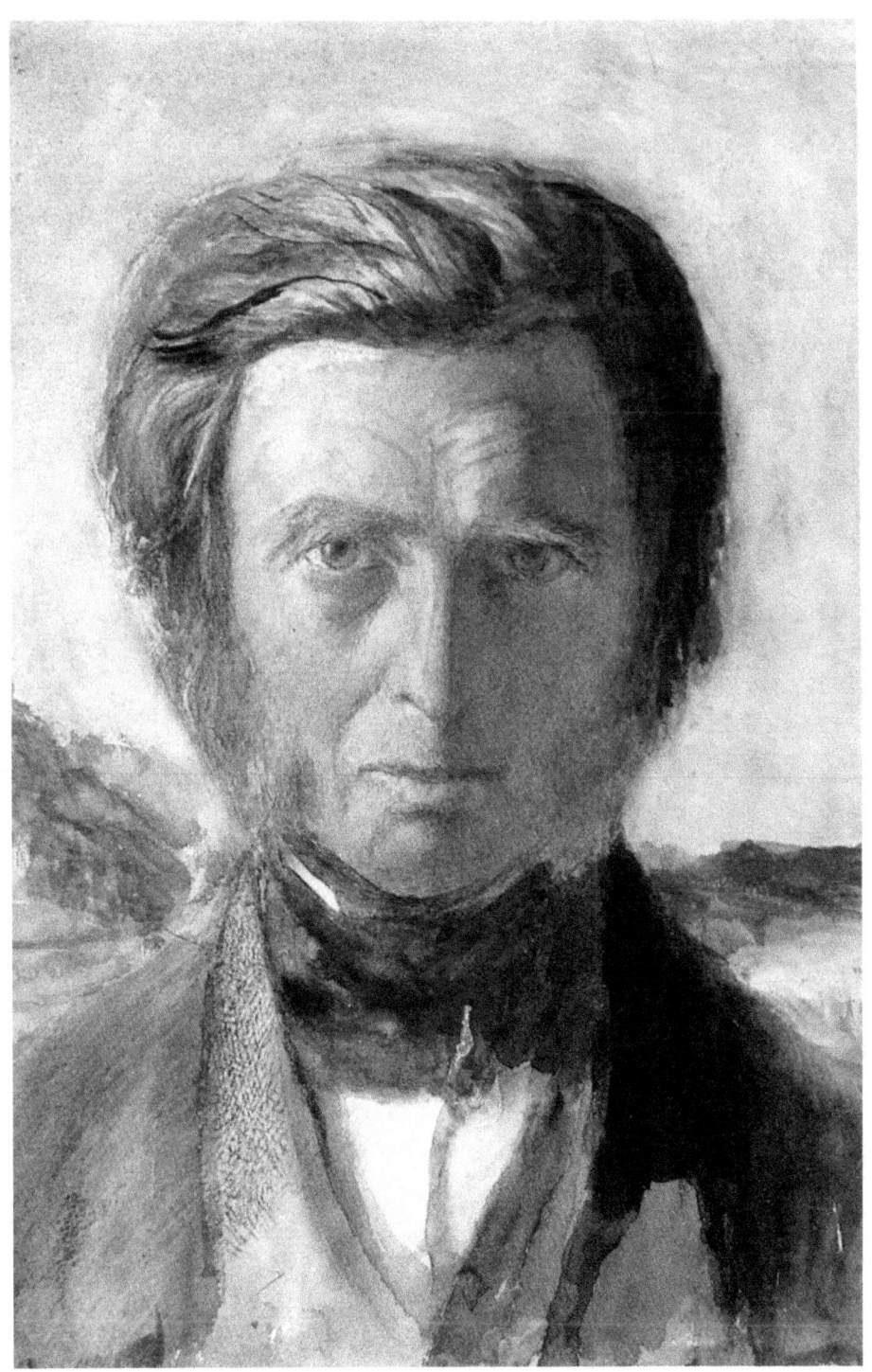

John Ruskin, Self-Portrait, 1875

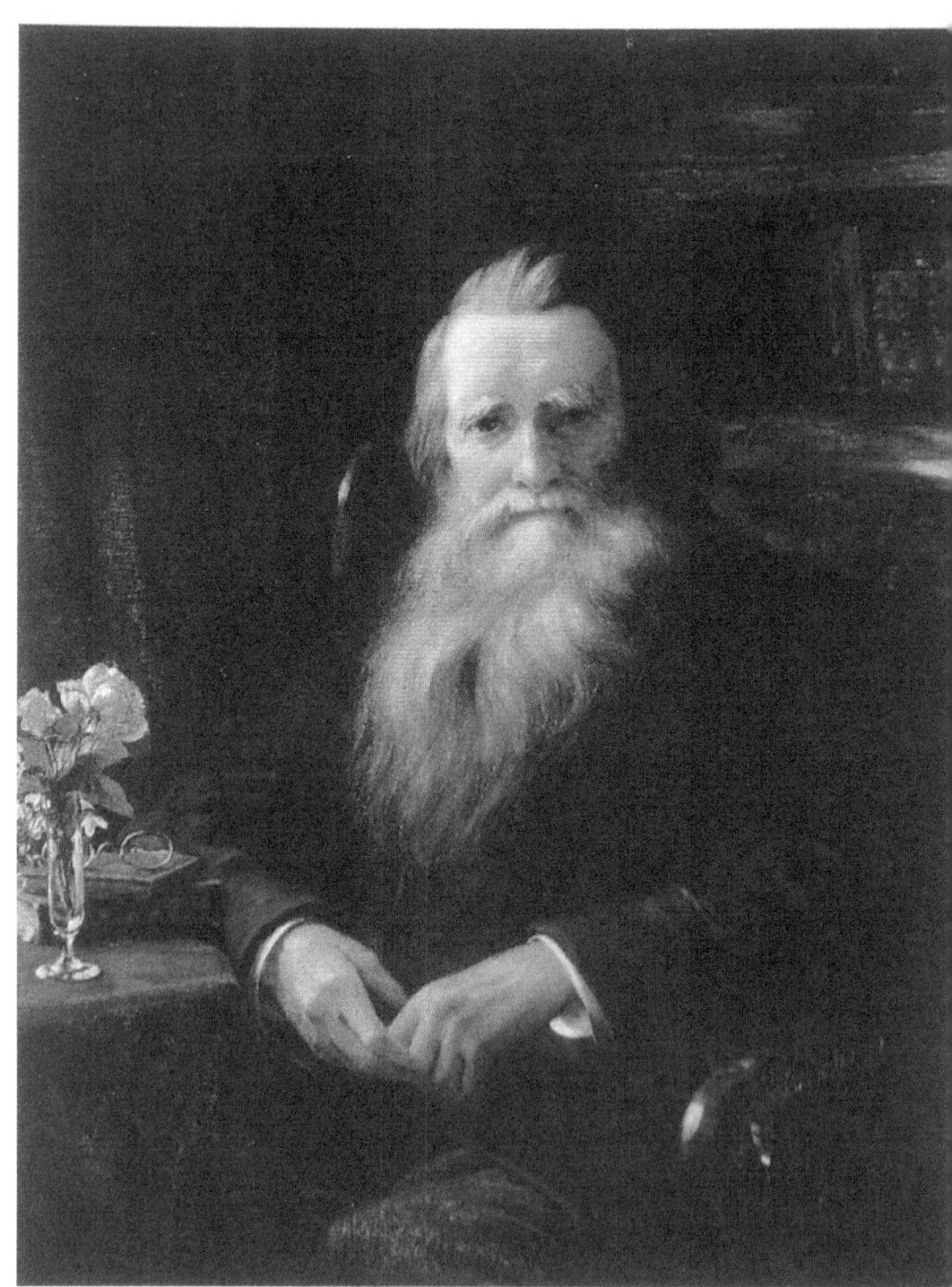

W.G. Collingwood,John Ruskin, 1897

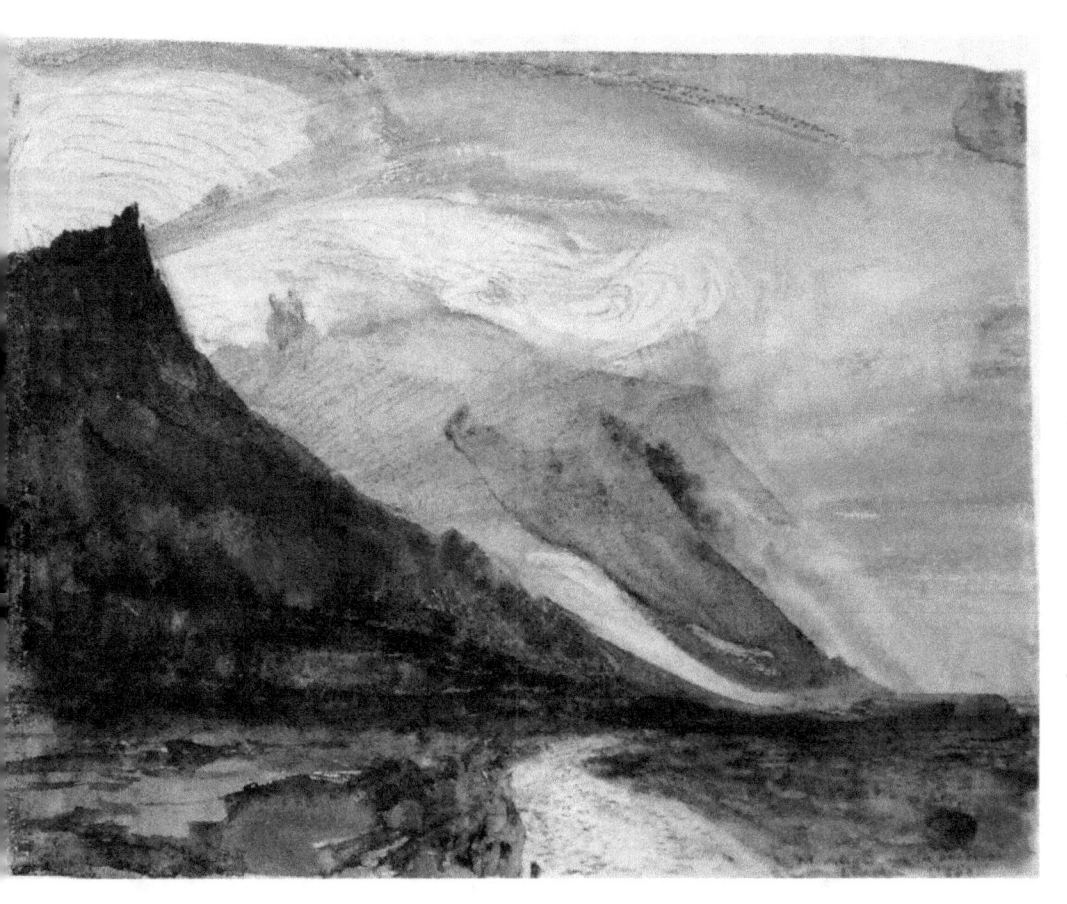

John Ruskin, Moonlight, Chamonix, 1888

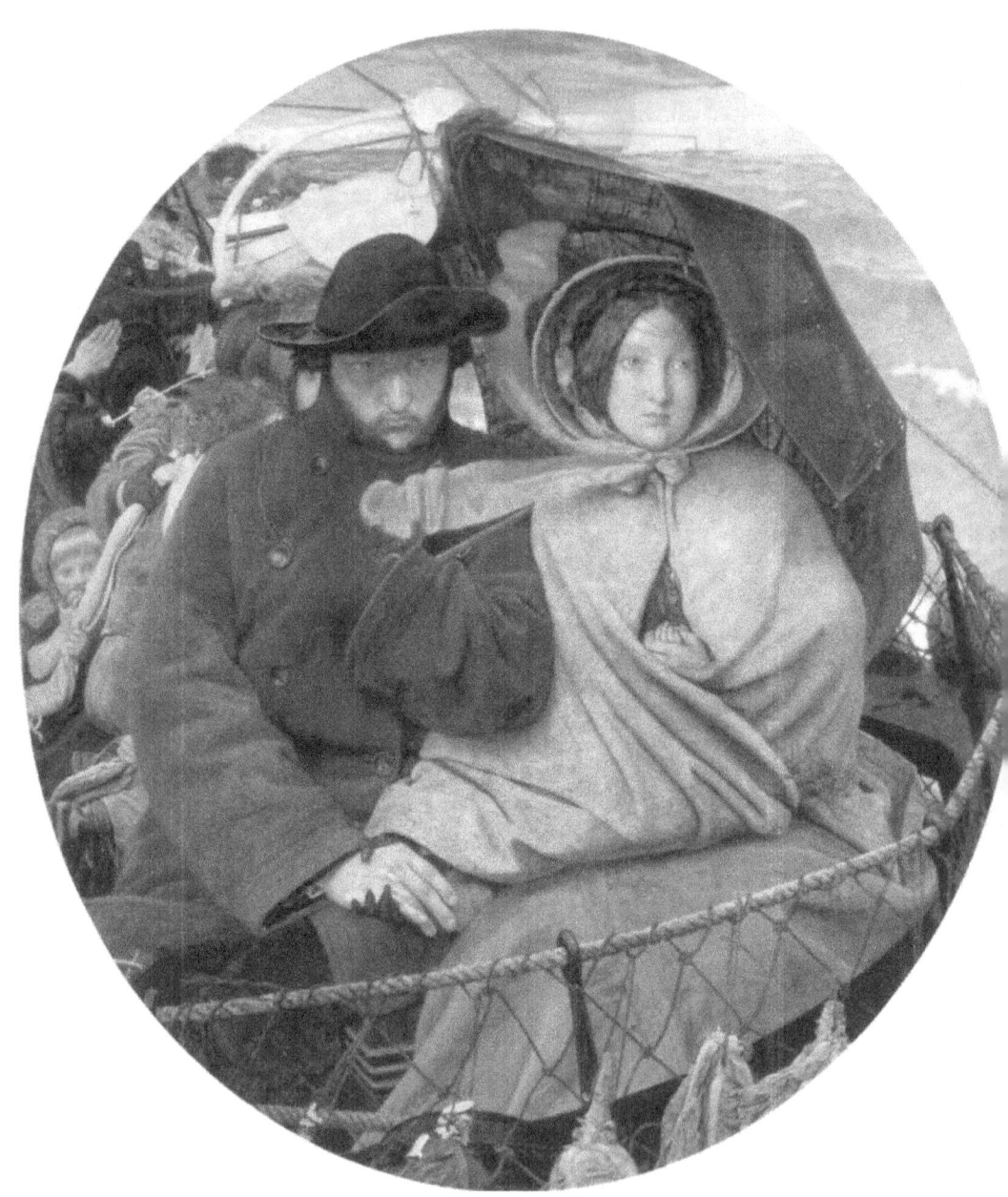

Ford Madox Brown, The Last of England, 1855,
Birmingham

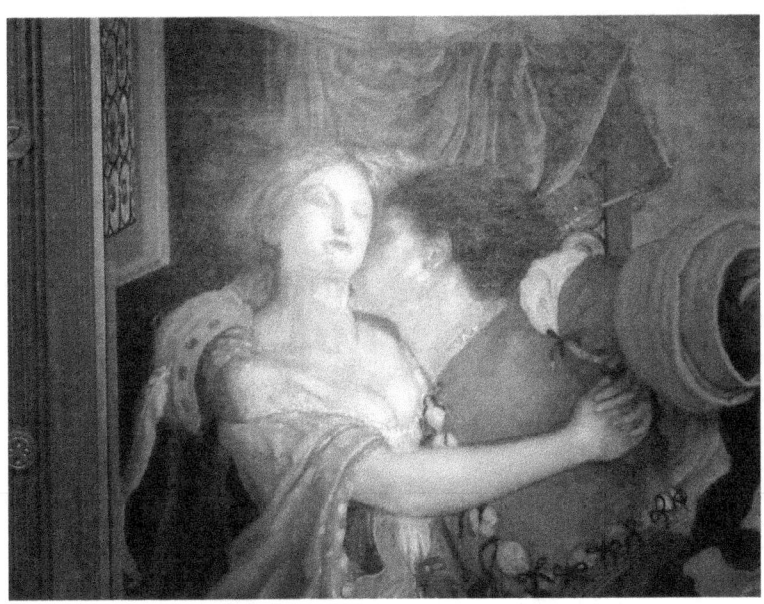

Ford Madox Brown, Romeo and Juliet, 1869-70, Delaware

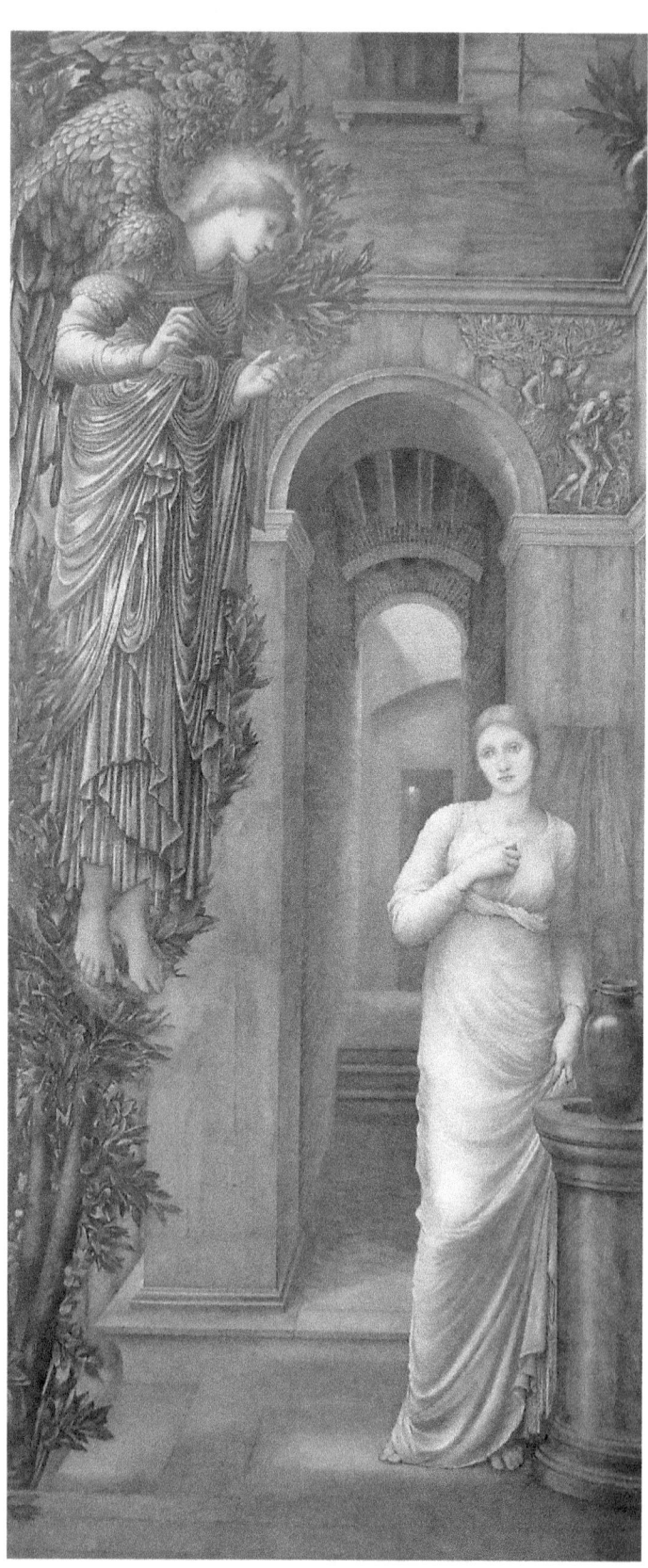

Edward Burne-Jones,
Annunciation, 1879

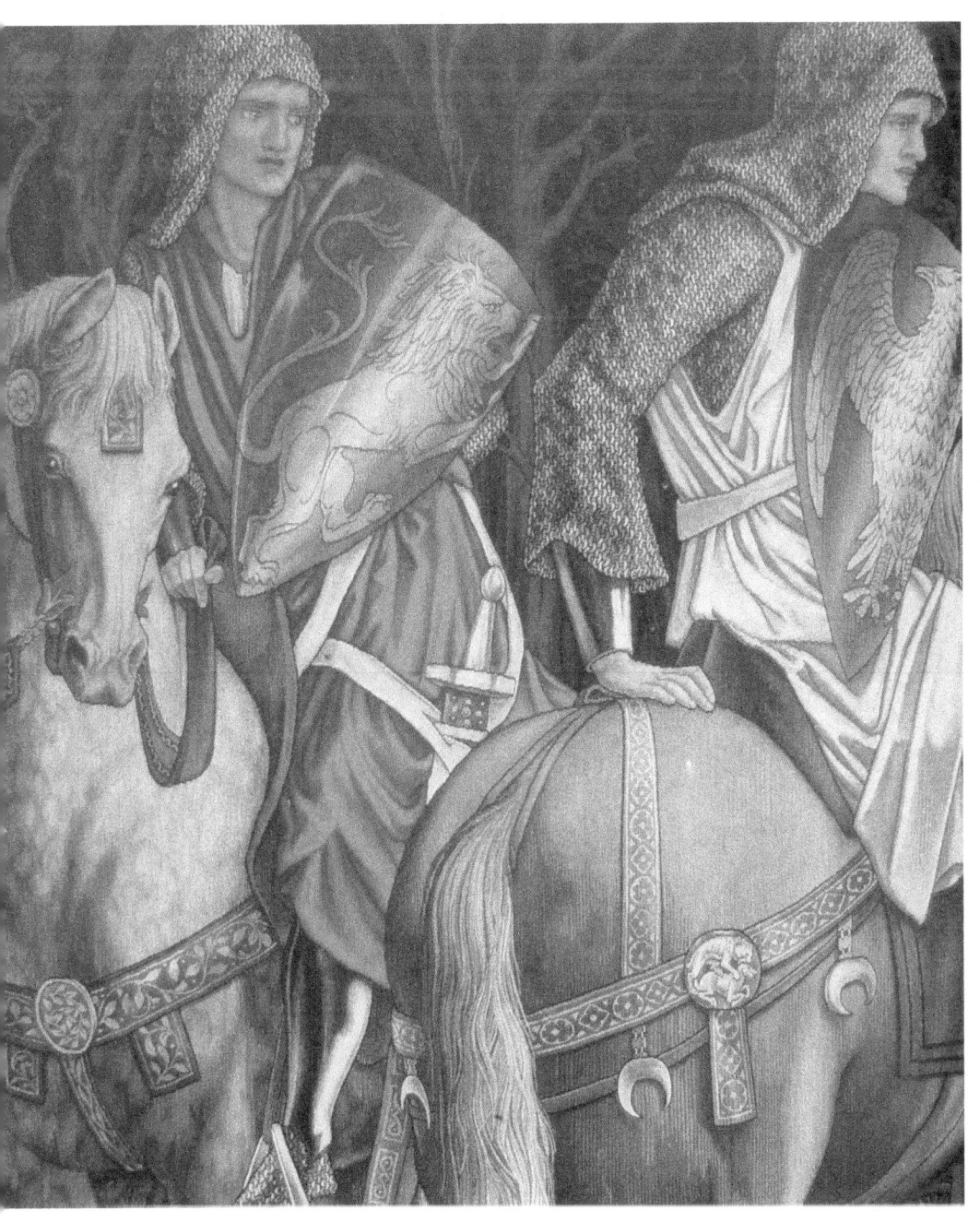

Edward Burne-Jones, The Fall of Lucifer, 1894, detail

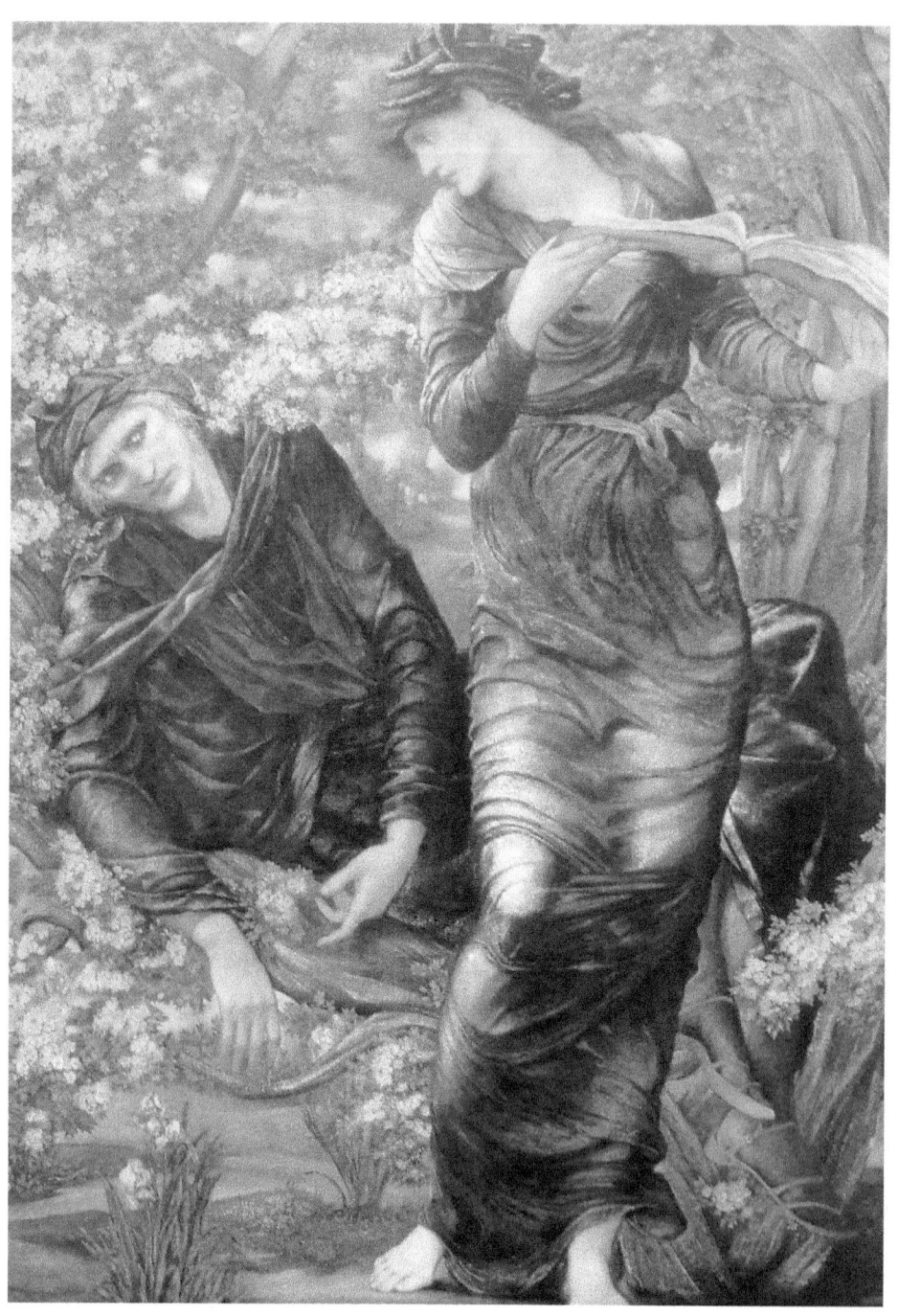

Edward Burne-Jones, The Beguiling of Merlin, 1874

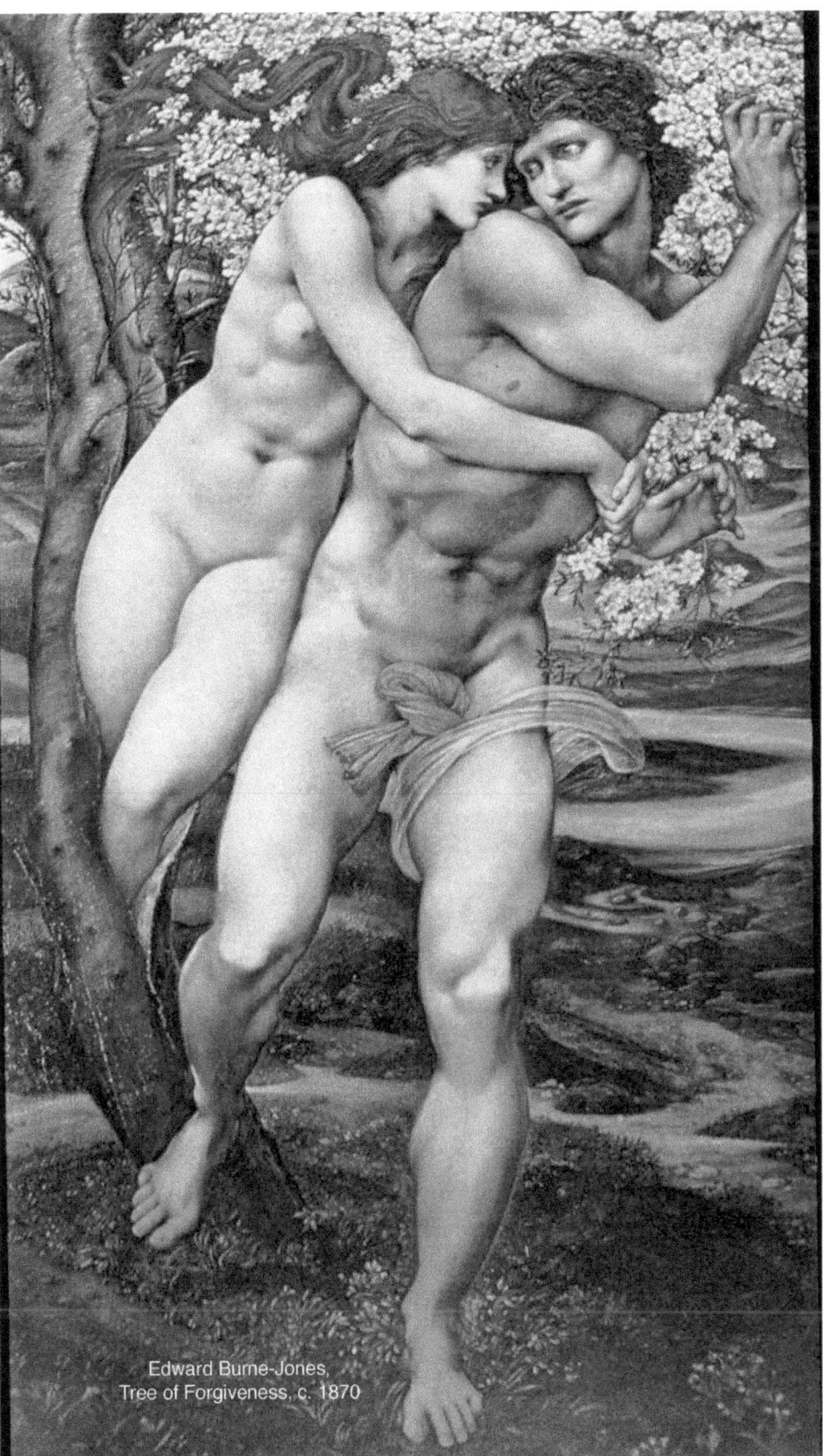

Edward Burne-Jones,
Tree of Forgiveness, c. 1870

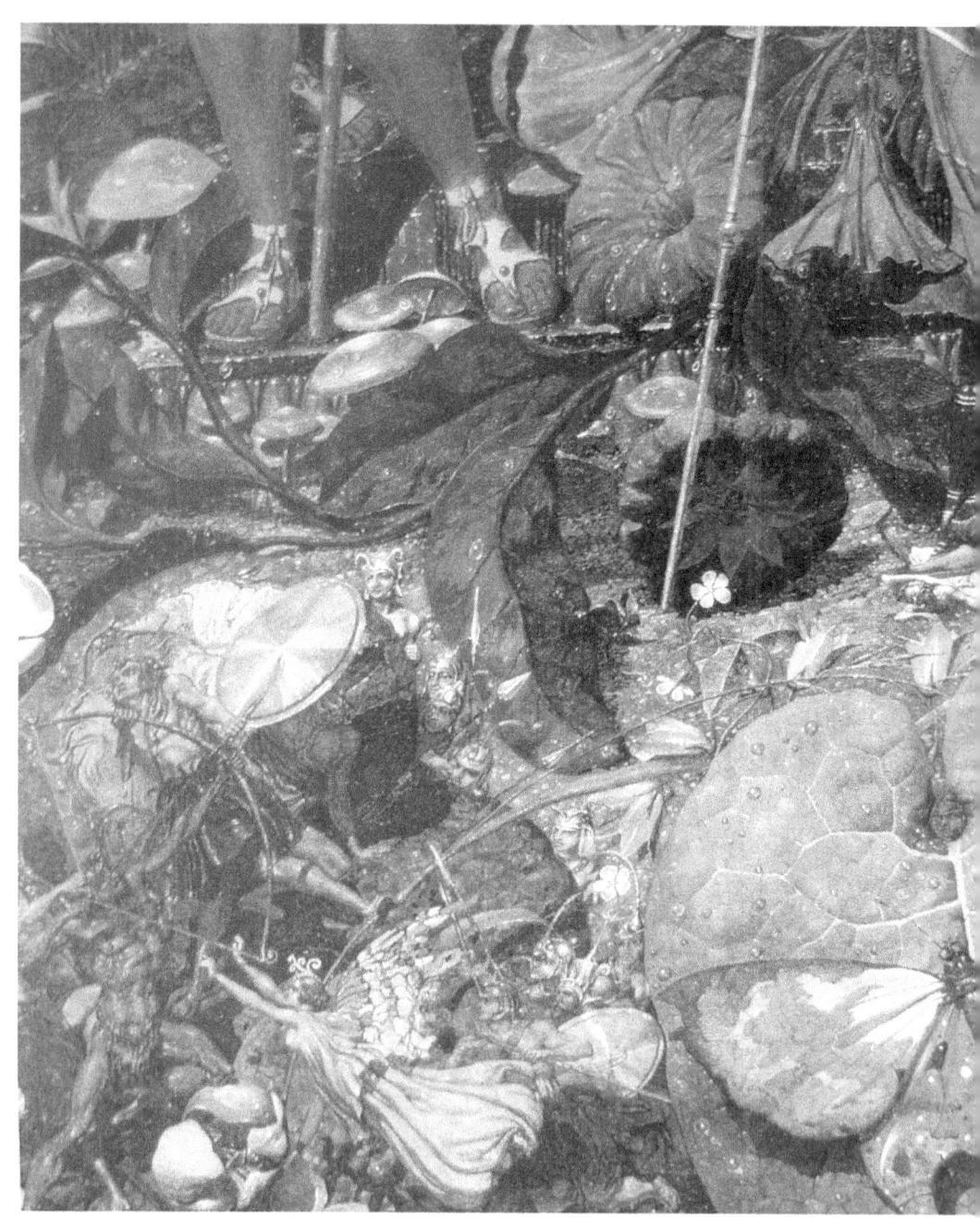

Richard Dadd, Contradiction: Oberon and Titania, 1854/ 58, detail

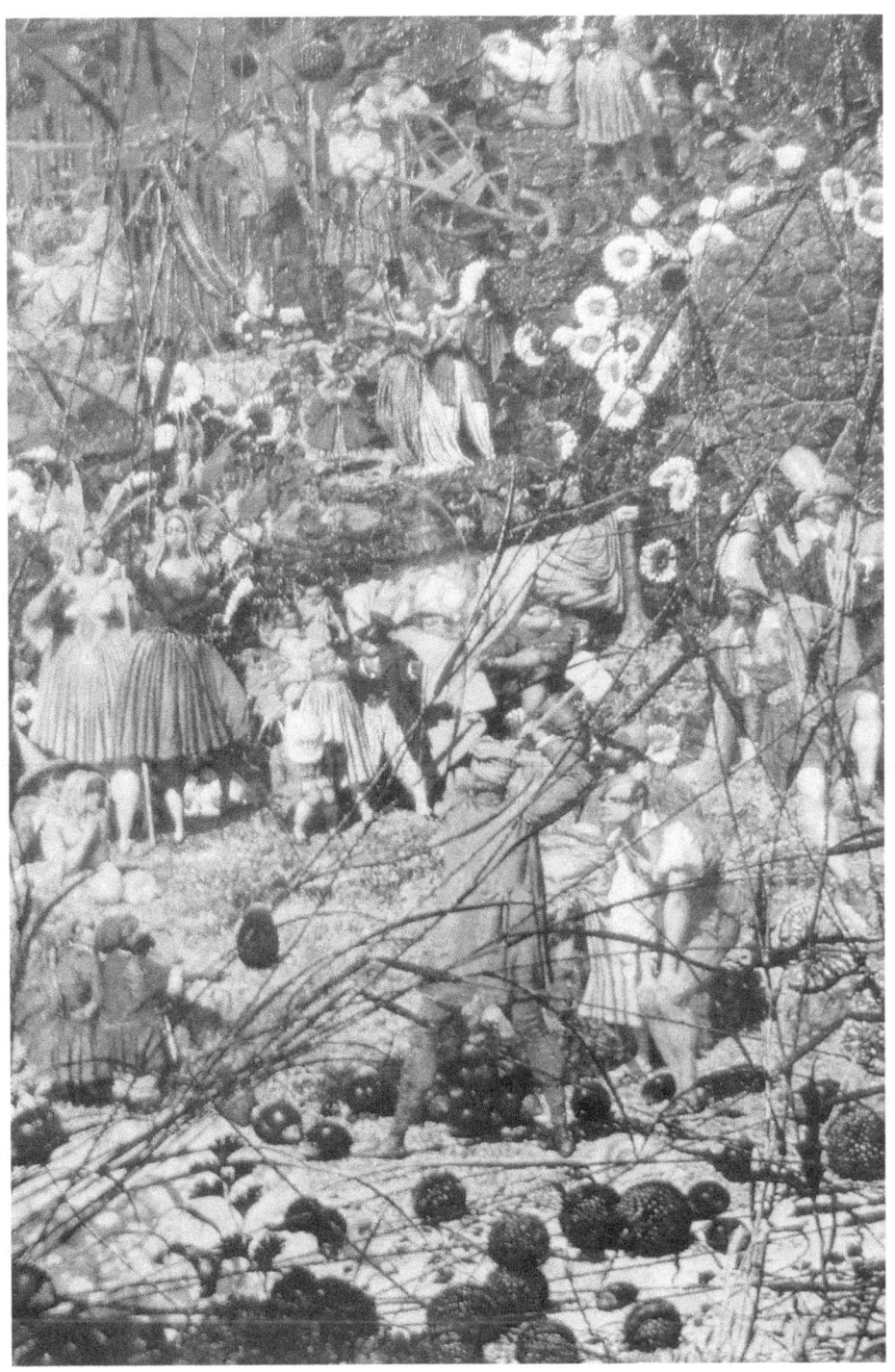

Richard Dadd, The Fairy-Feller's Master-Stroke, Tate, London

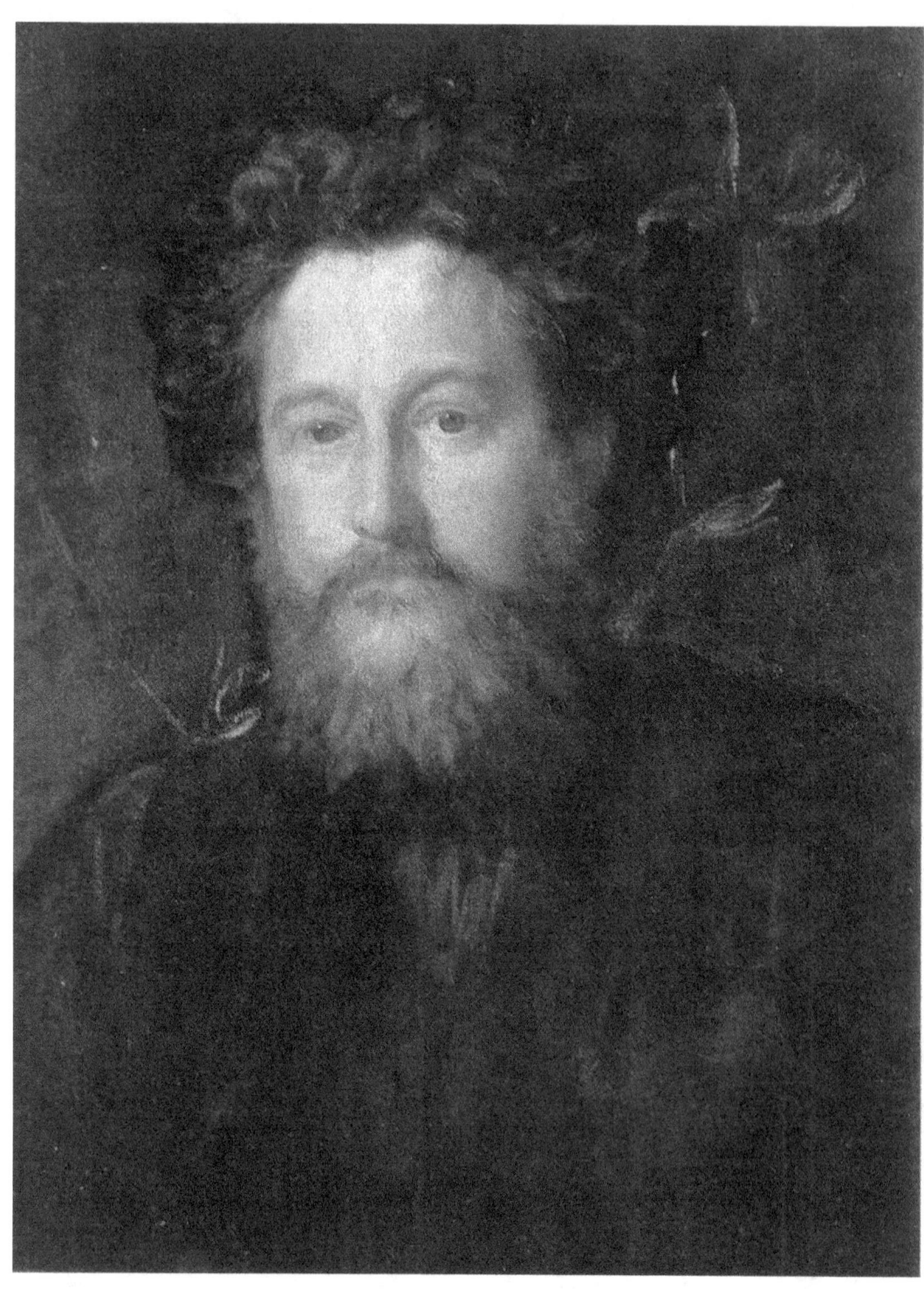

George Frederic Watts, Portrait of William Morris, 1870

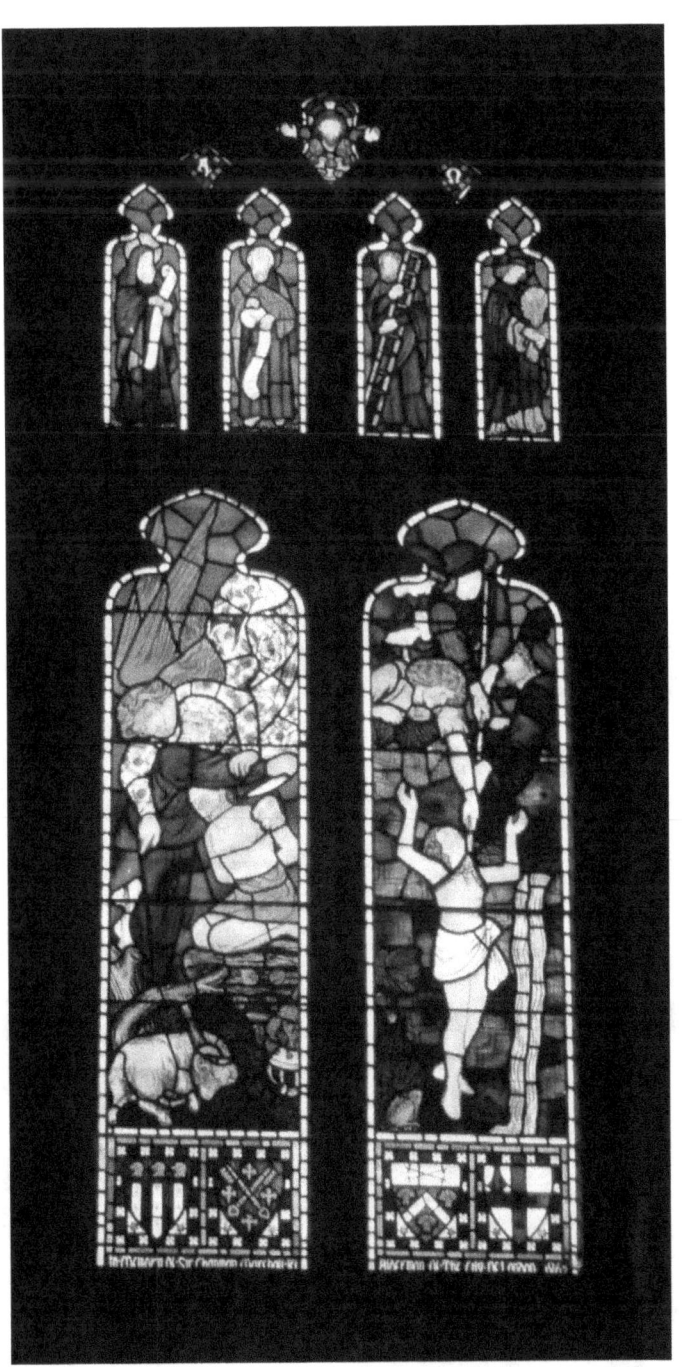

William Morris, Glass, Peterborough Cathedral, 1870

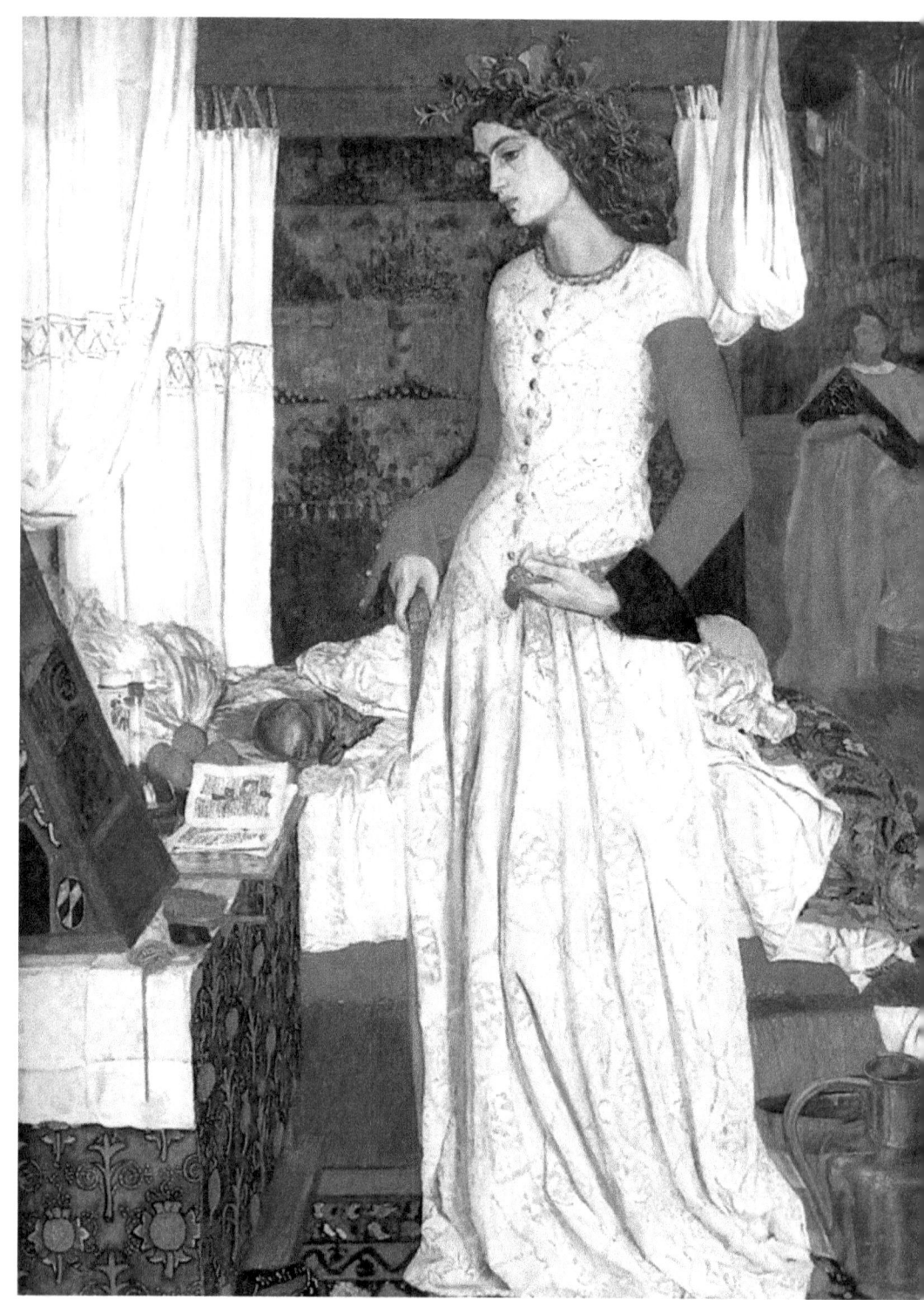

William Morris, La Belle Iseult, 1858, Tate Gallery

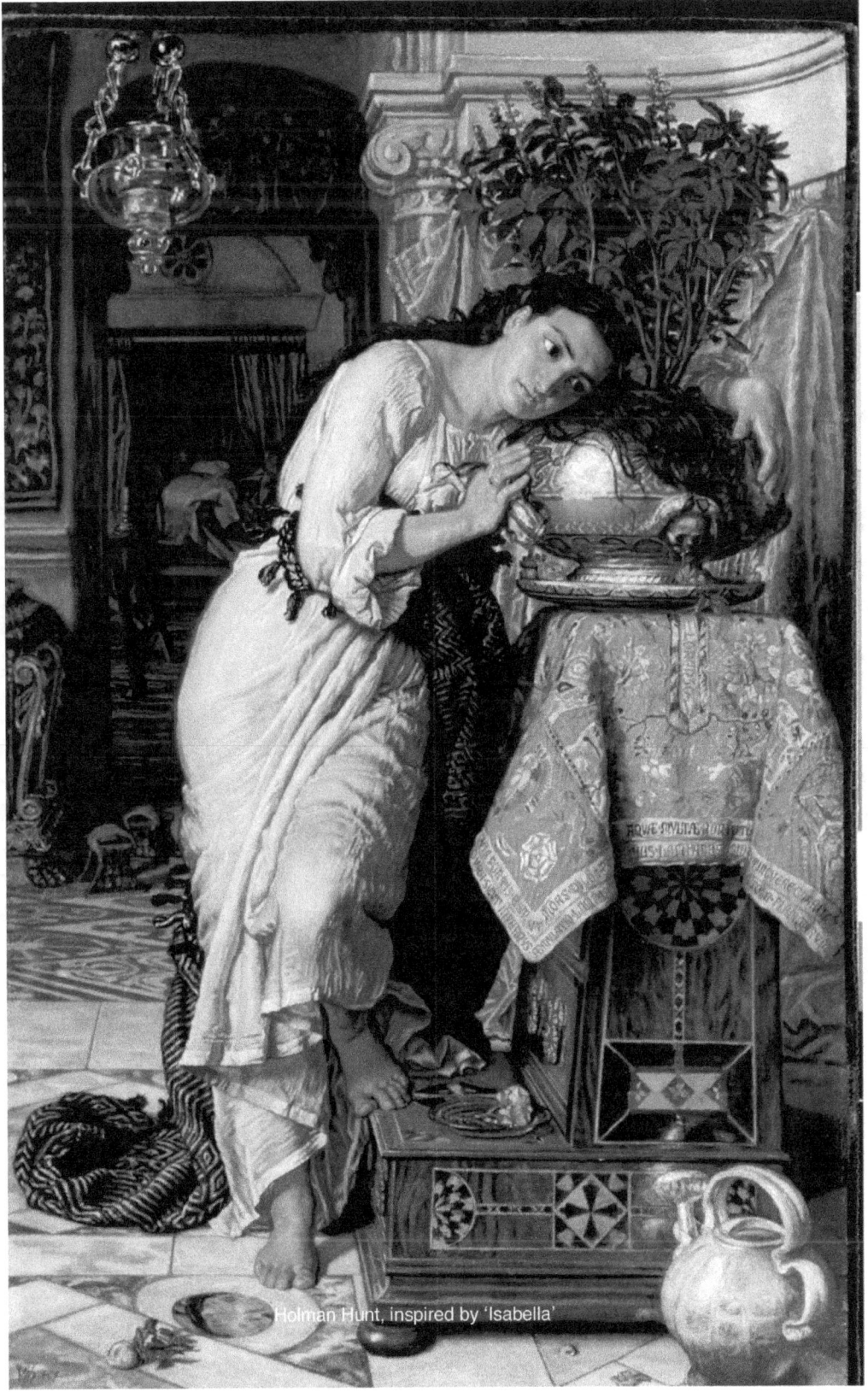

Holman Hunt, inspired by 'Isabella'

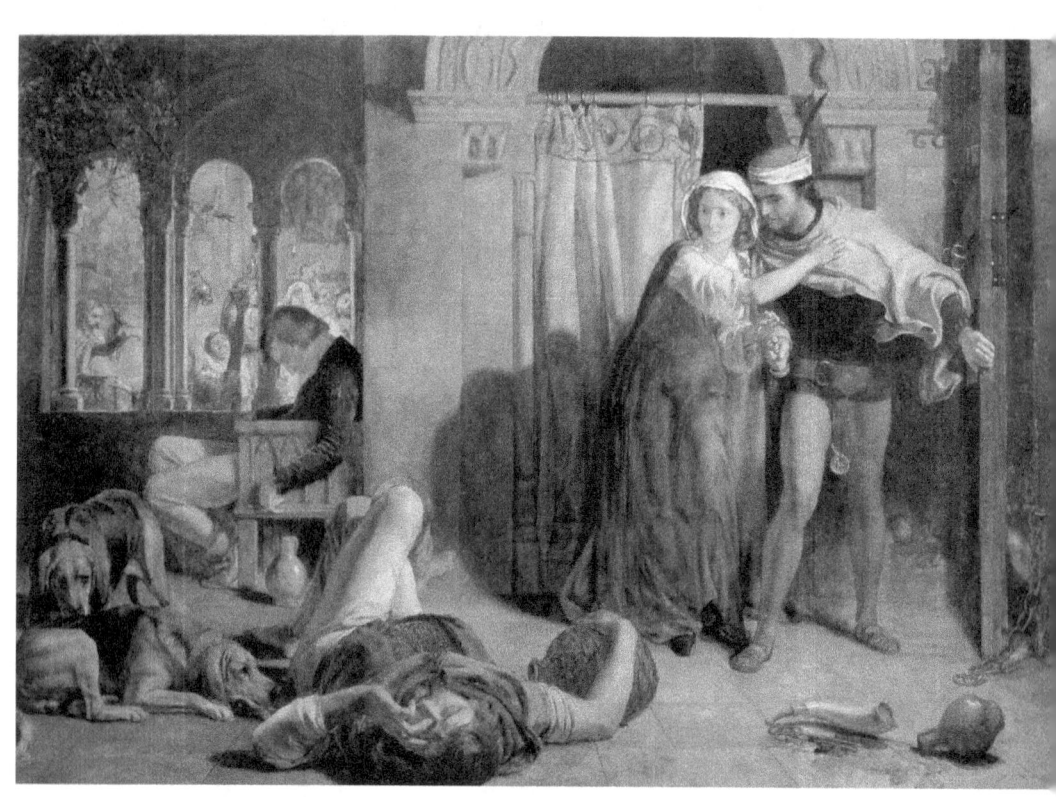

John William Holman Hunt, The Flight of Madeline and Porphyro

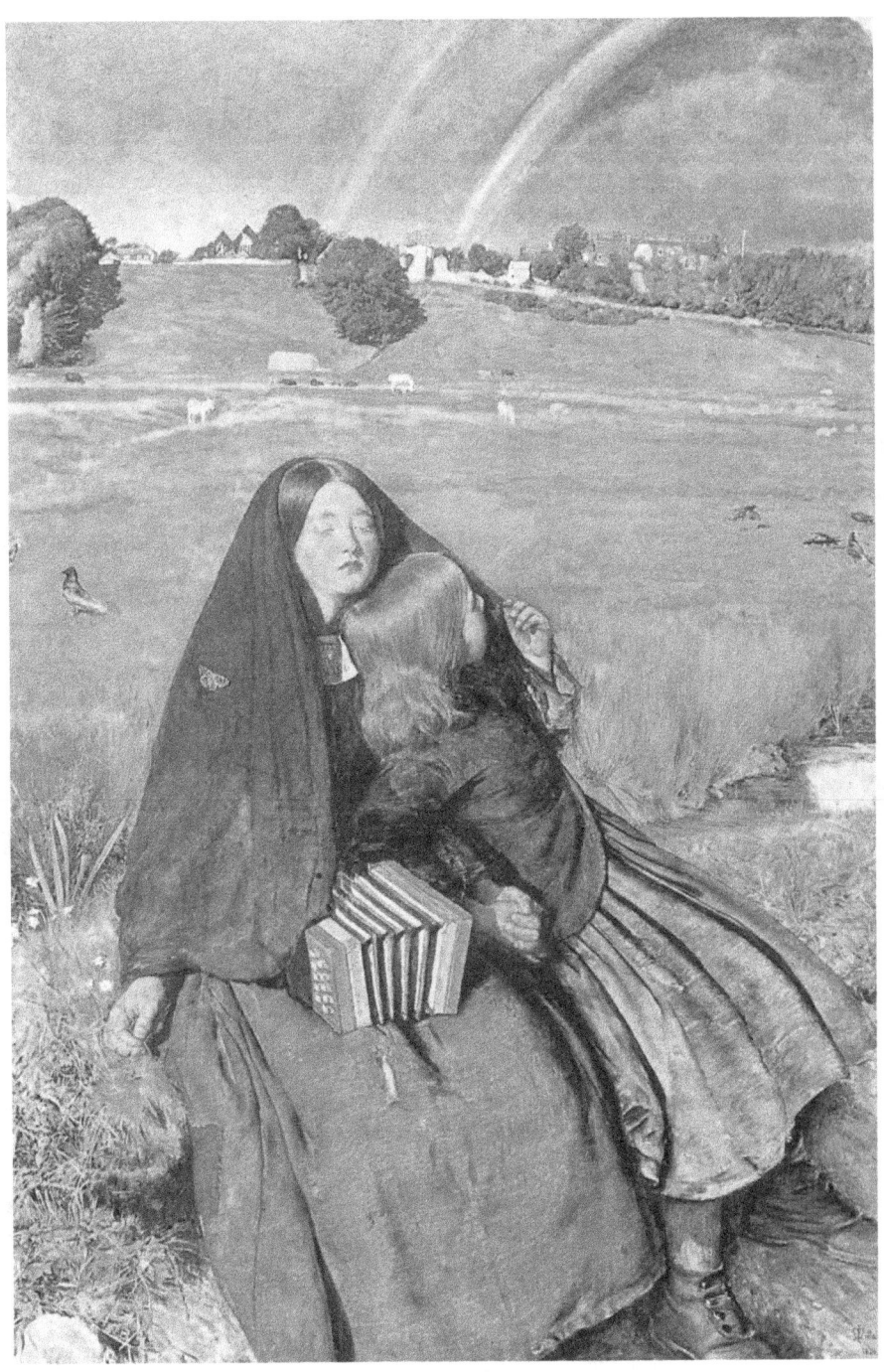

John Everett Millais, Blind Girl, 1885, Birmingham

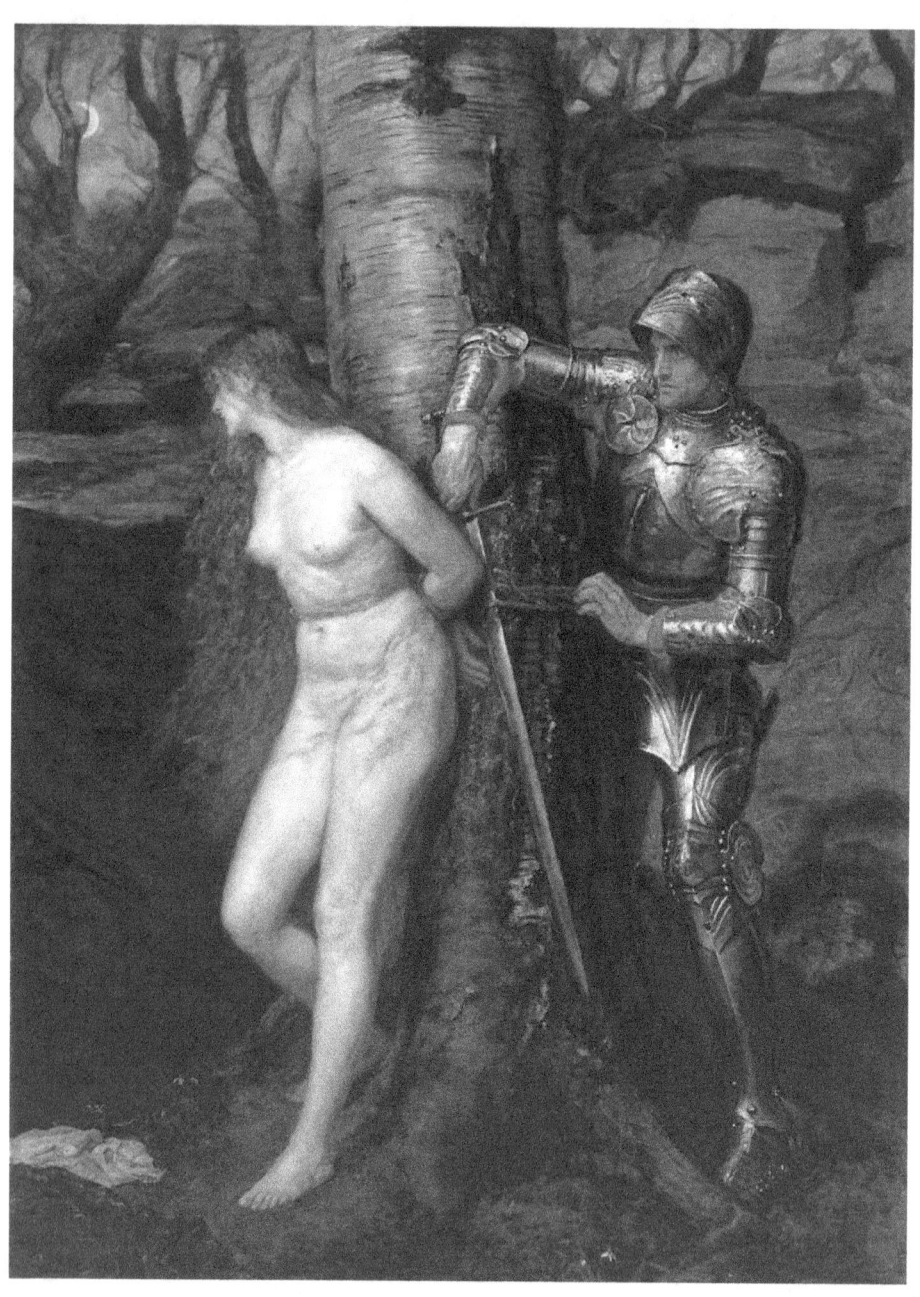

John Everett Millais, The Knight Errant, 1870, Tate, London

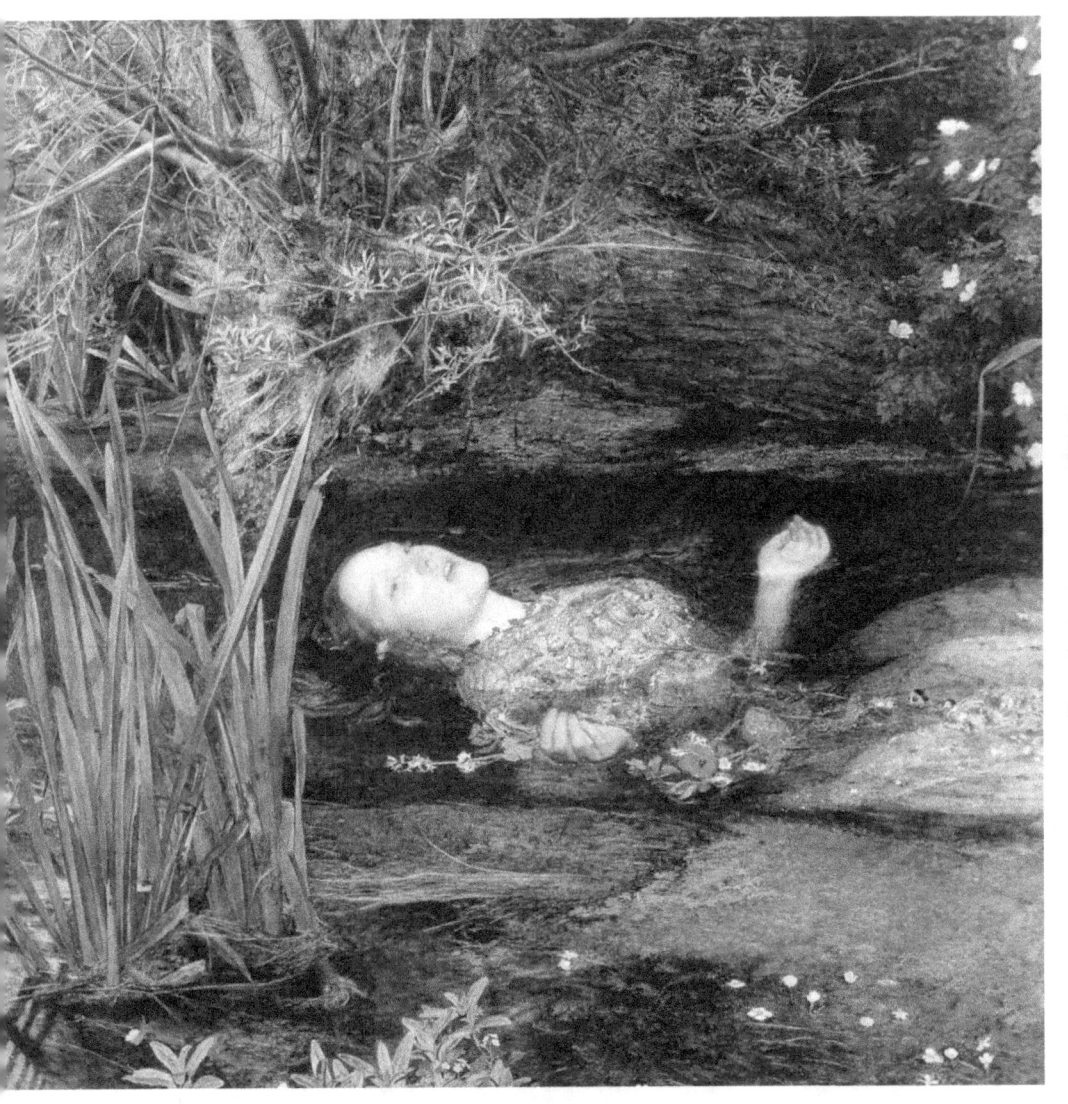

John Everett Millais, Ophelia.

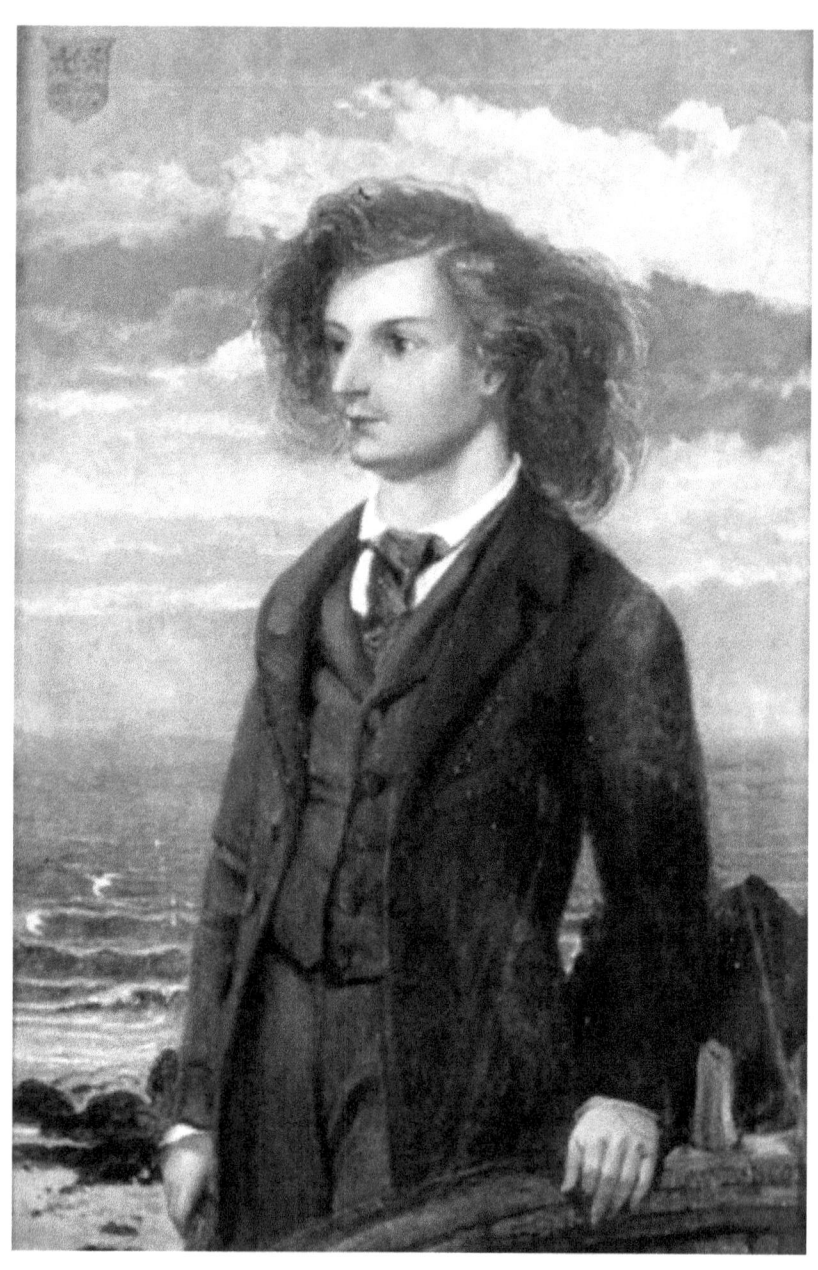

William Bell Scott, Algernon Charles Swinburne, Baillol College

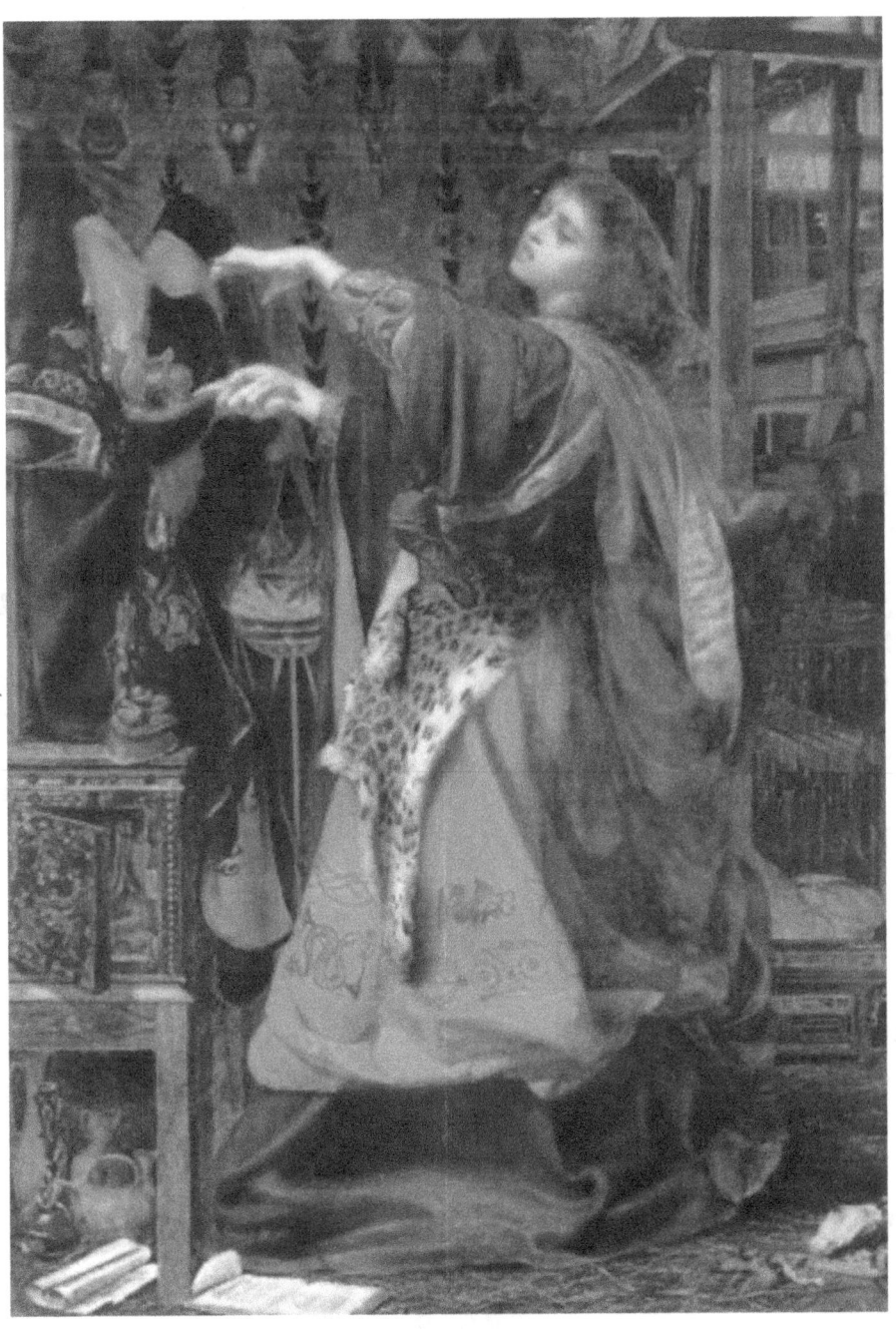

Frederick Sandys, Morgan le Fay, 1863-34, Birmingham

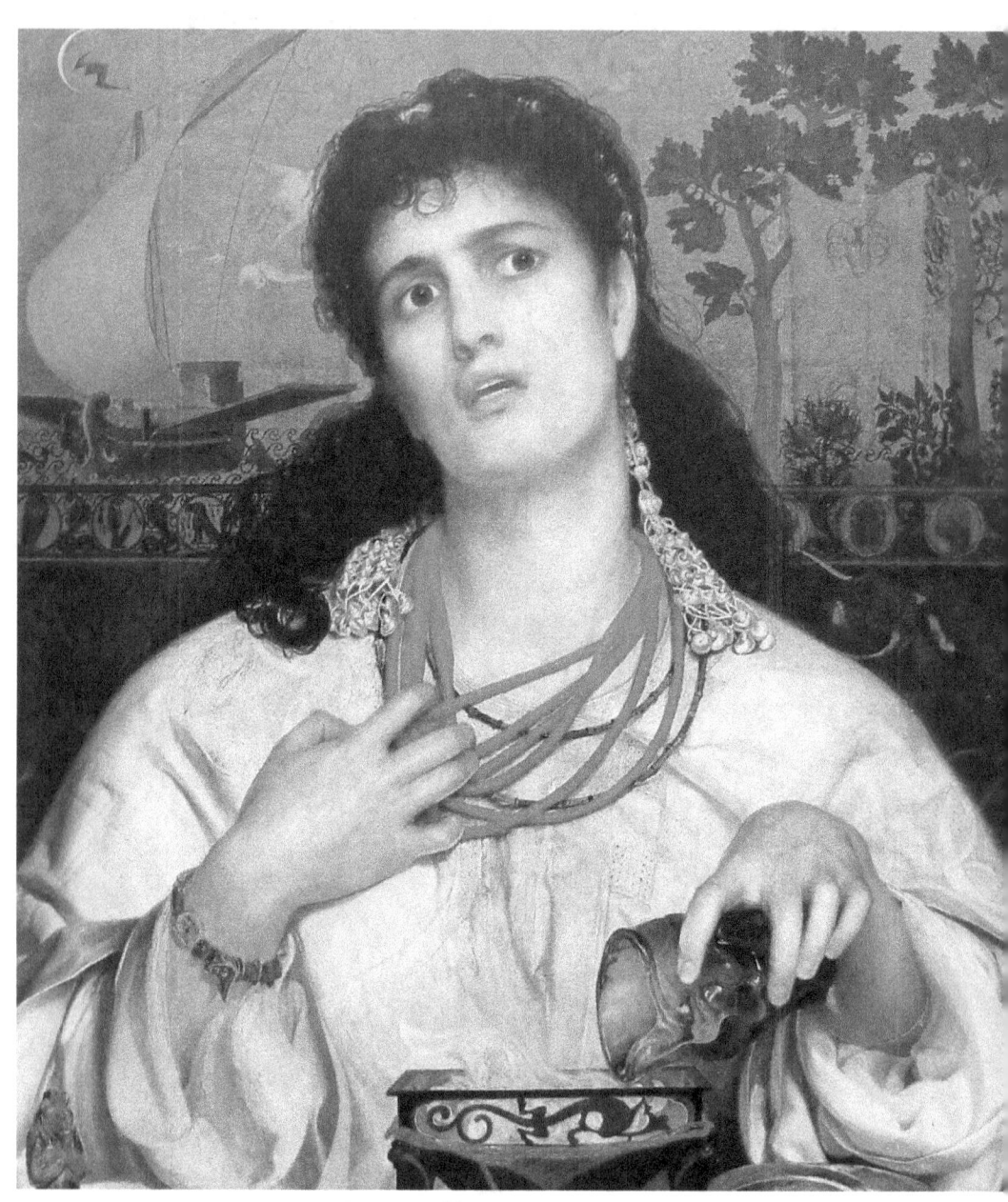

Frederick Sandys, Medea, 1868

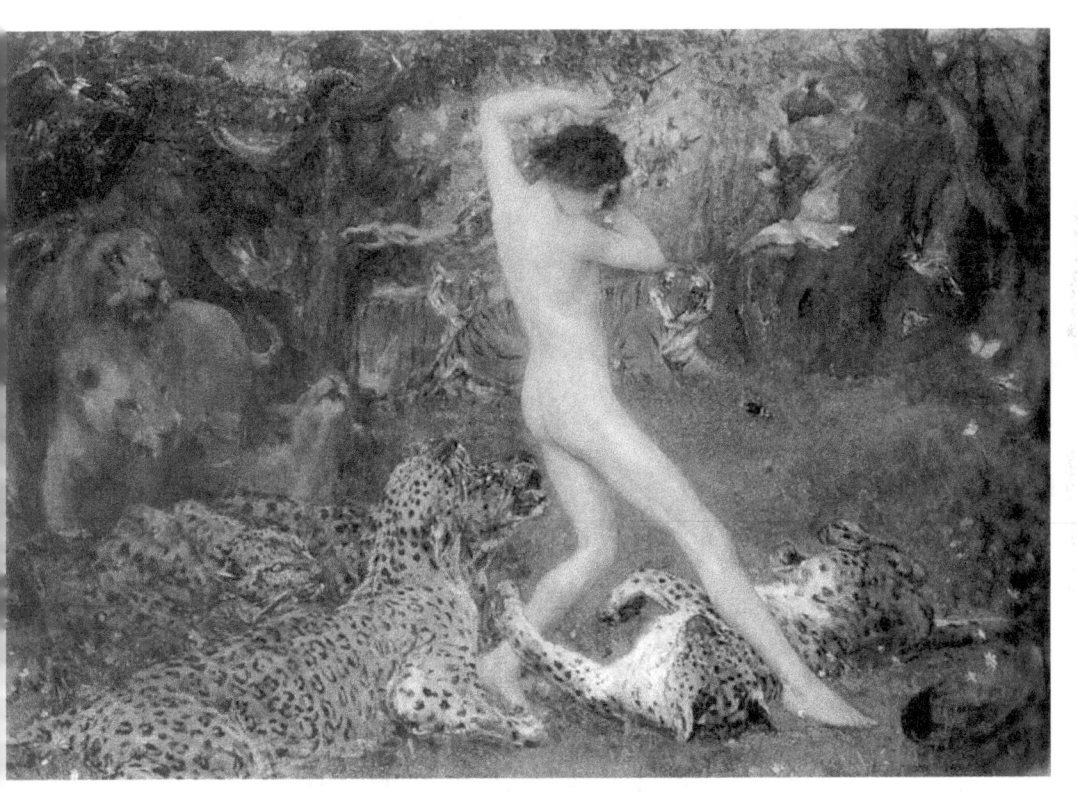

John Macallan Swan, Orpheus, 1896

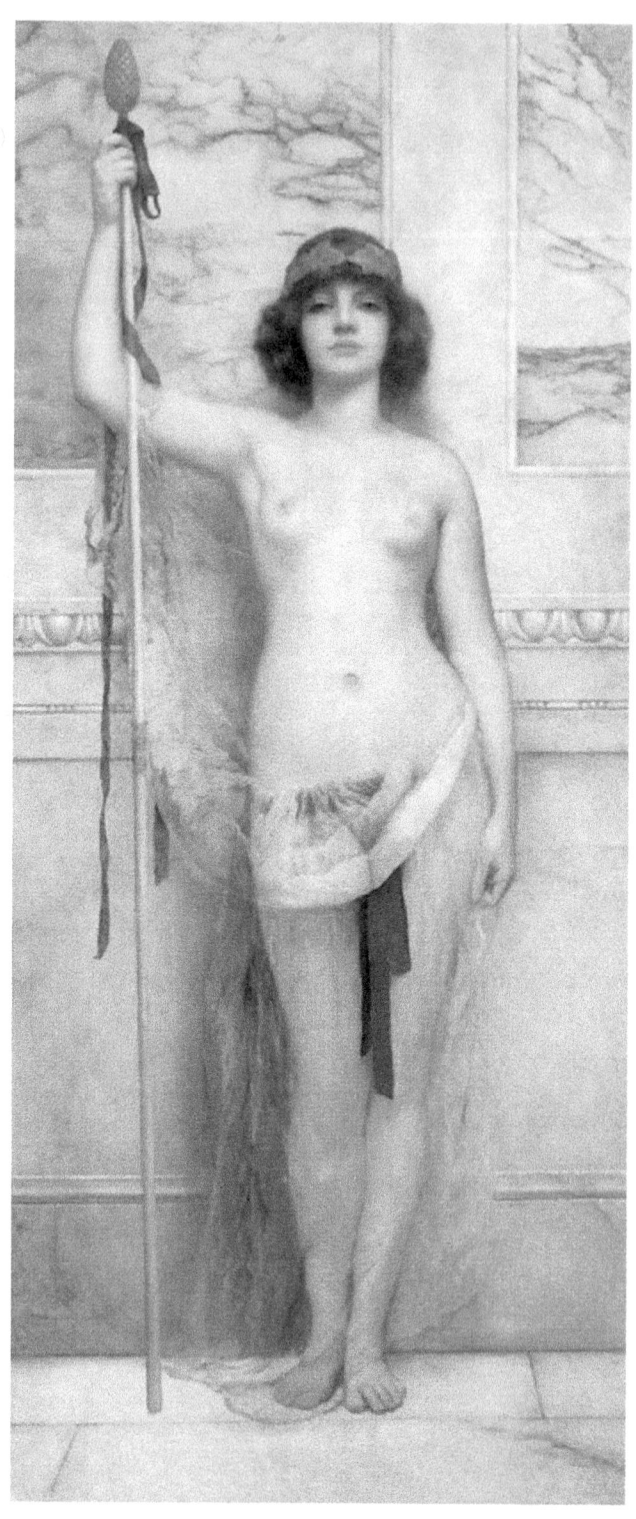

John Godward, A Priestess, 1893

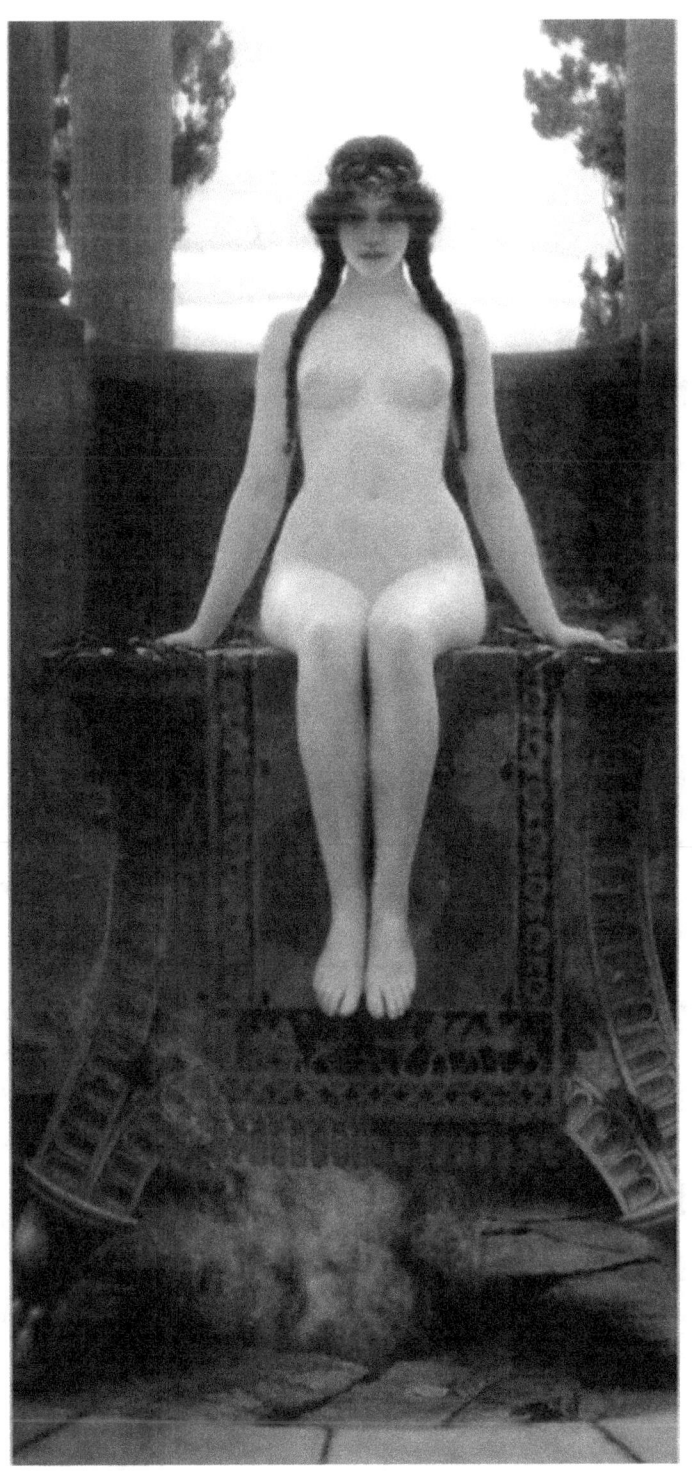

John Godward, The Delphic Oracle, 1899

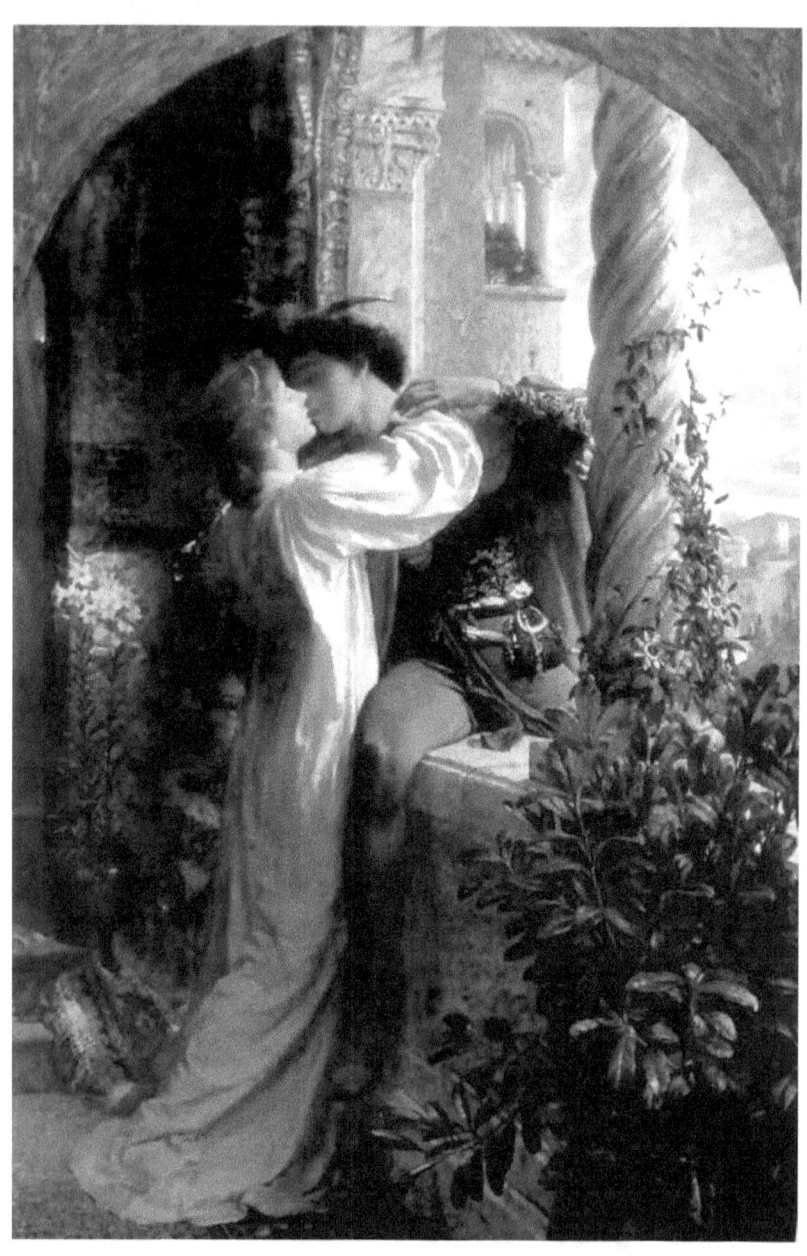

Francis Dicksee, Romeo & Juliet, 1884, Southampton

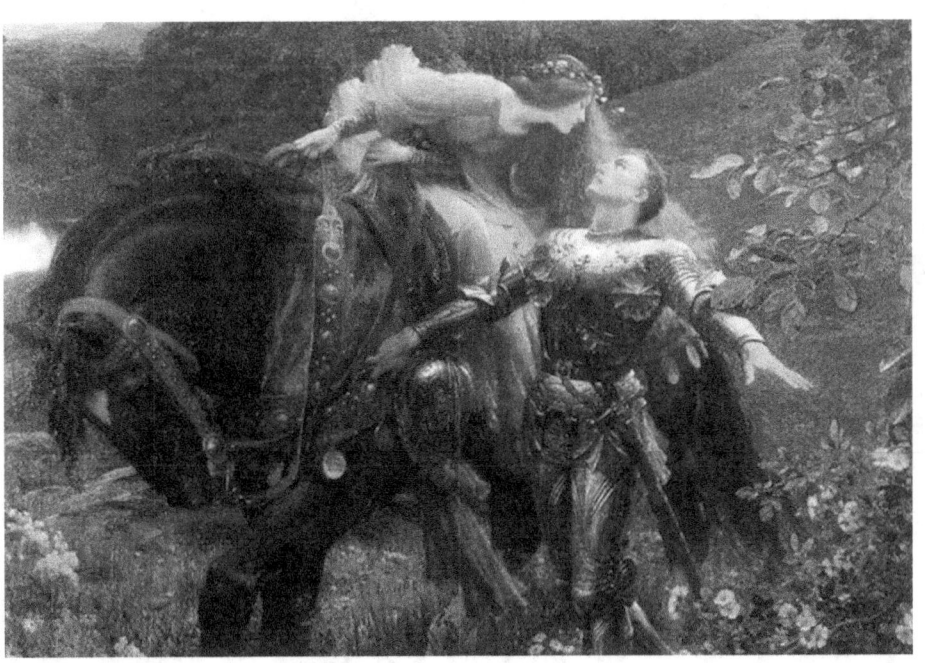

Sir Francis Dicksee, 'La Belle Dame Sans Merci'

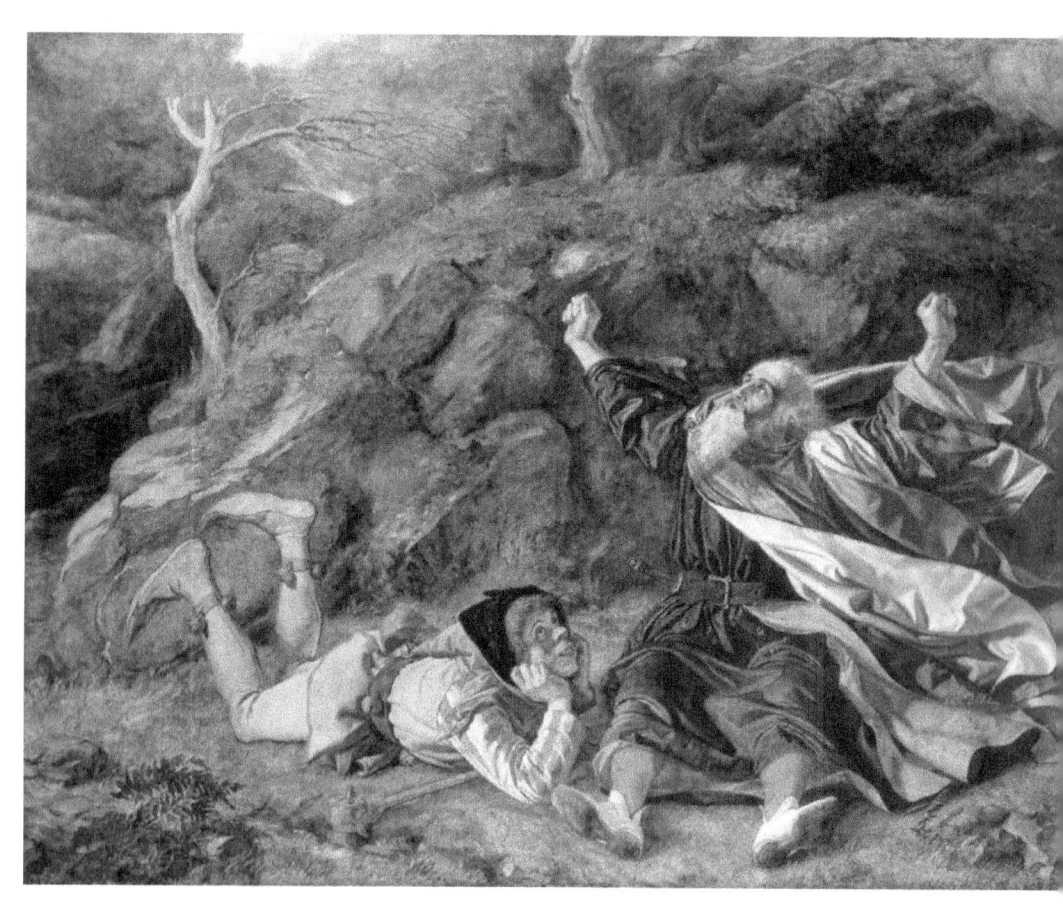

William Dyce, King Lear and the Fool In the Storm, 1851, Edinburgh

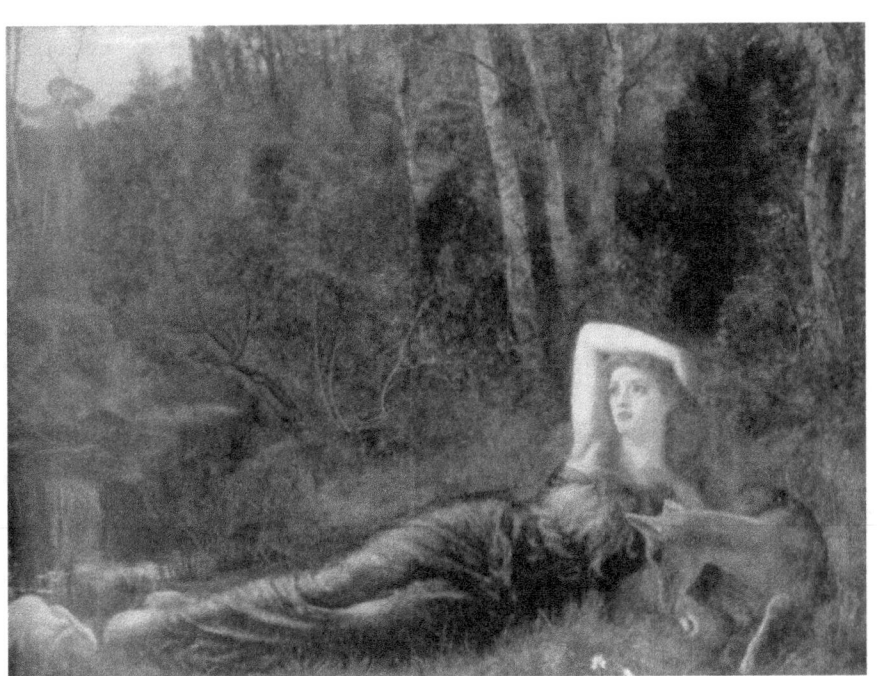

Arthur Hughes, Endymion

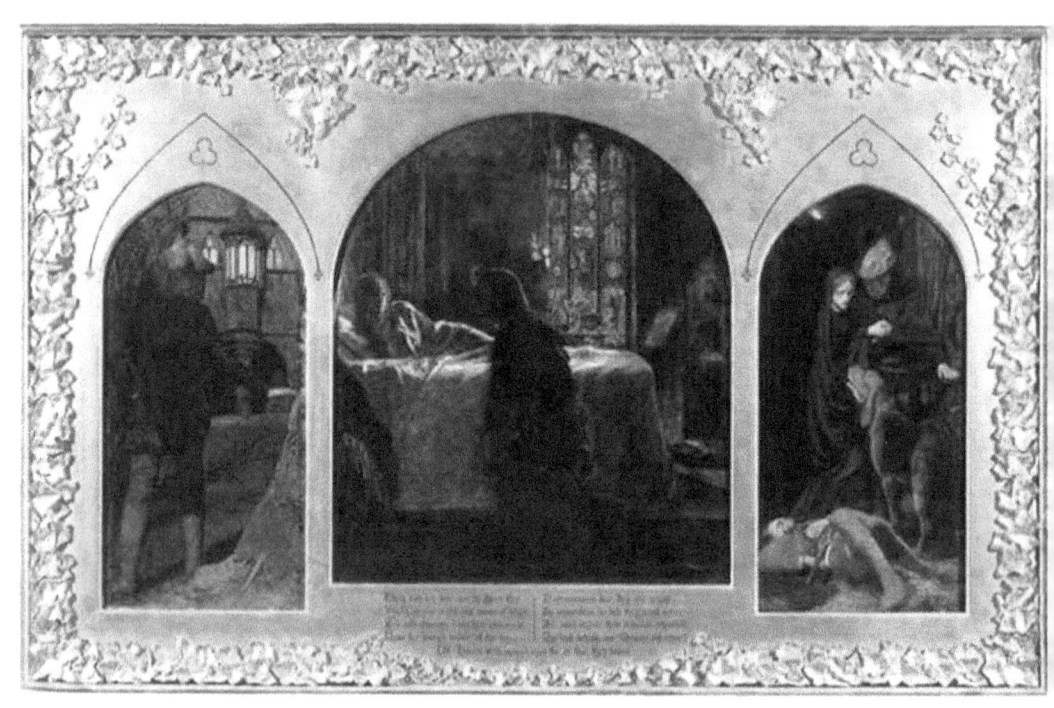

Arthur Hughes, The Eve of St Agnes

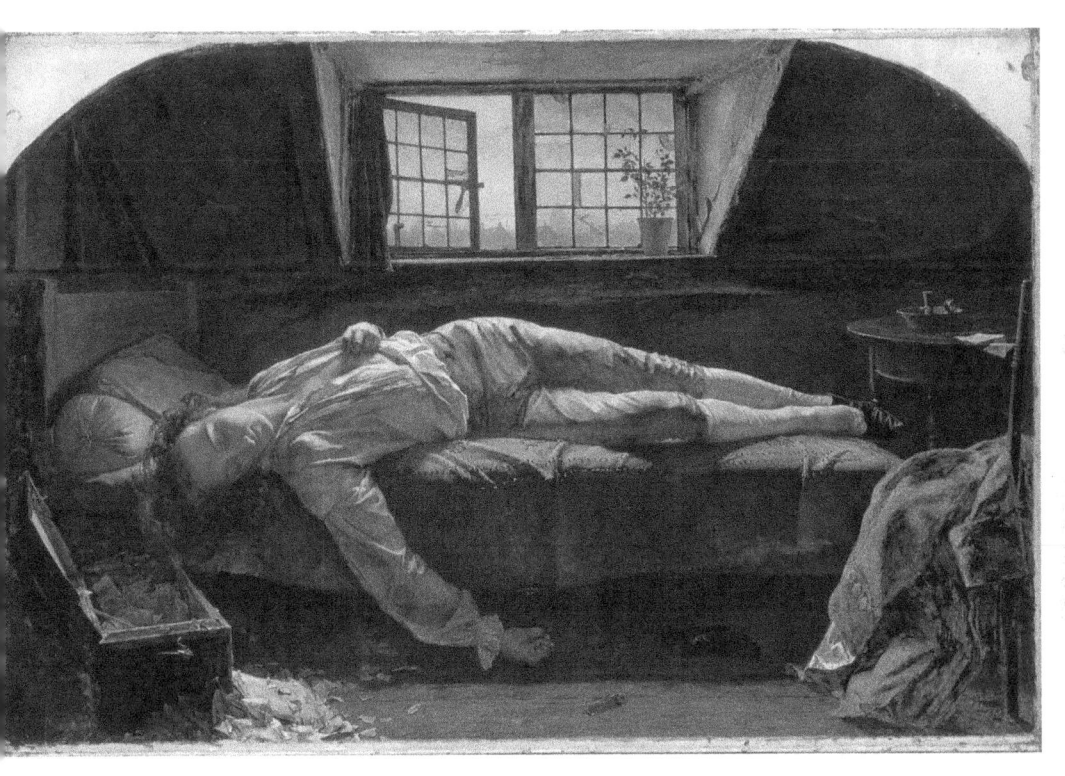

Henry Wallis, Chatterton, 1856, Tate Britain

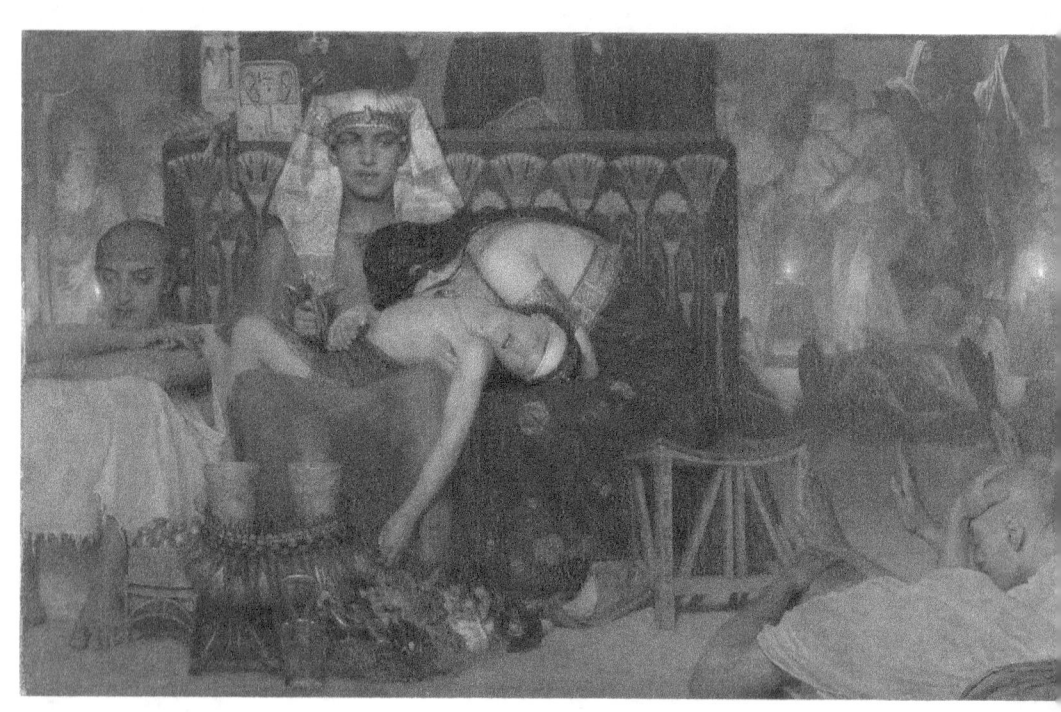

Lawrence Alma-Tadema,
The Death of the Pharaoh's Firstborn Son, 1872,
Rijksmuseum, Amsterdam

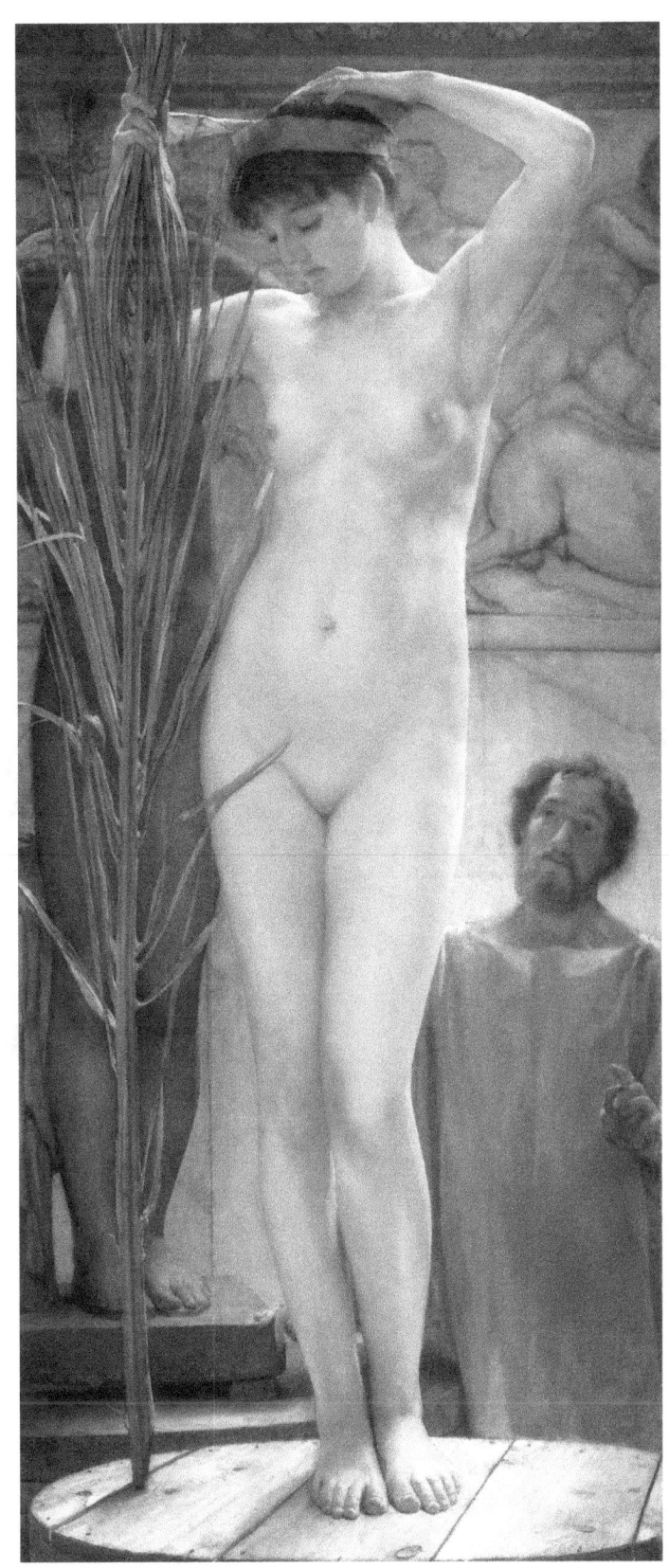

Lawrence
Alma-Tadema,
A Sculptor's Model,
1877, private
collection

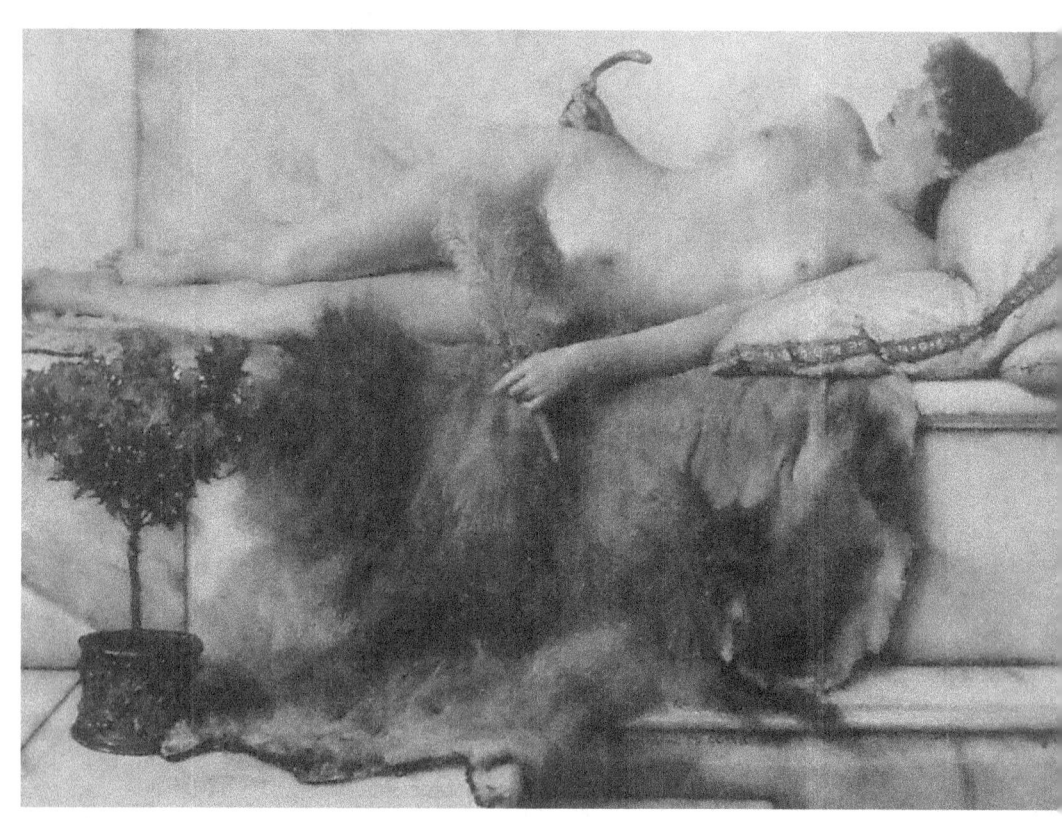

Lawrence Alma-Tadema, In the Tepidarium, 1881,
Lady Lever Art Gallery, Liverpool

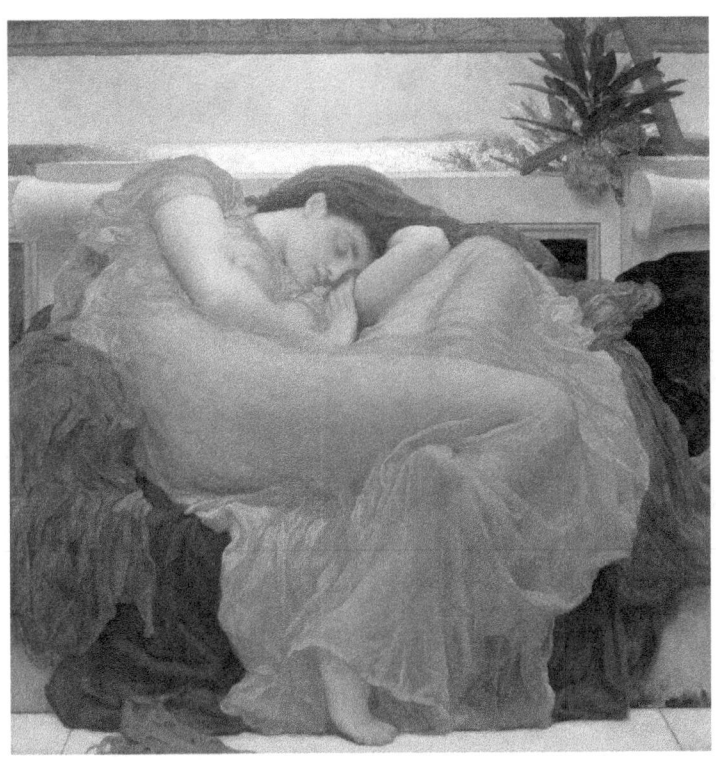

Lord Leighton, Flaming June, 1895, Puerto Rico

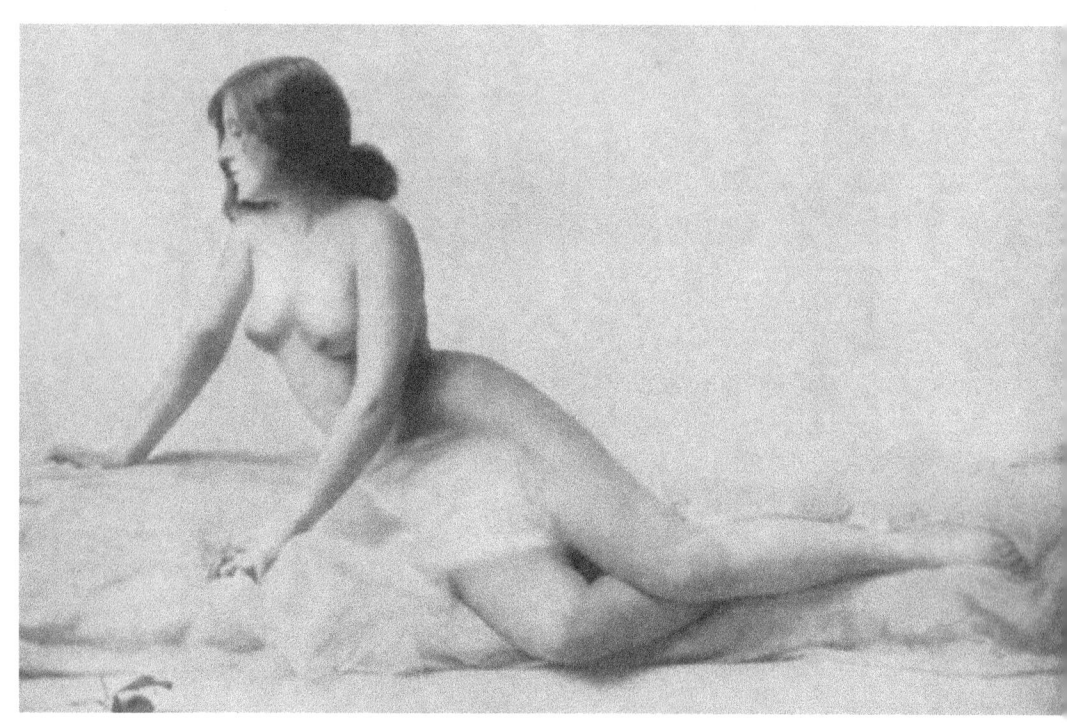

Frederick Armstrong, Greek Slave,
1909, drawn from Lord Leighton

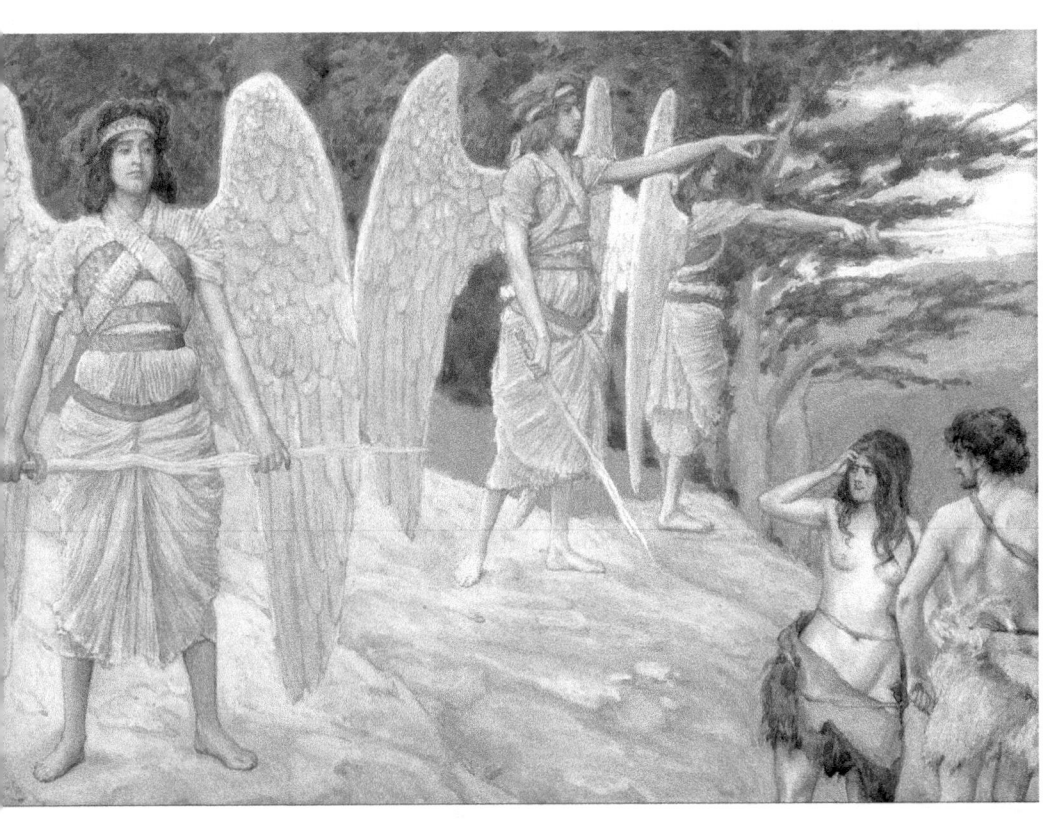

James Tissot, Adam and Eve Driven From Paradise, Jewish Museum, NYC

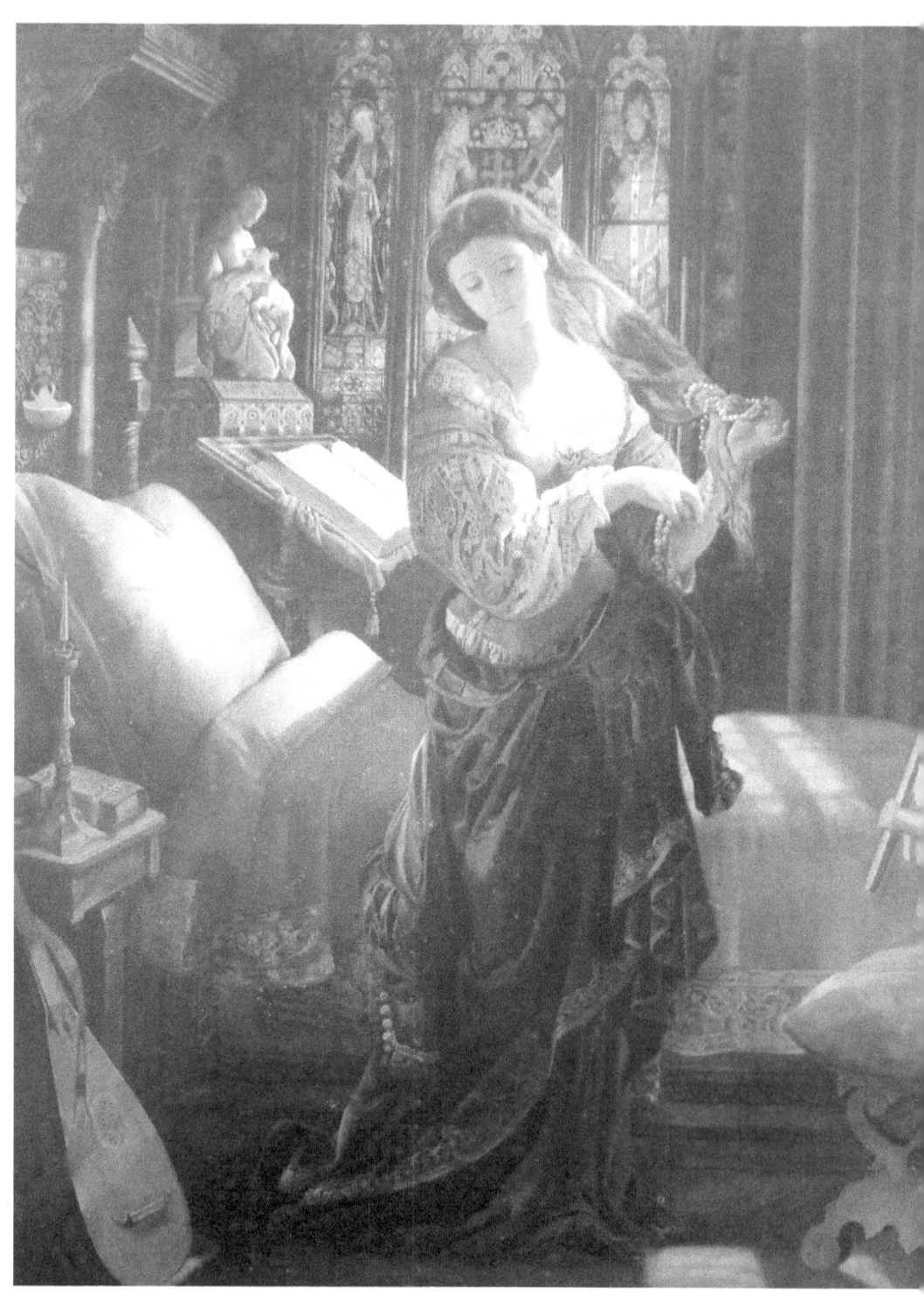

Daniel Maclise, Madeline After Prayer, 1868, Walker Art Gallery

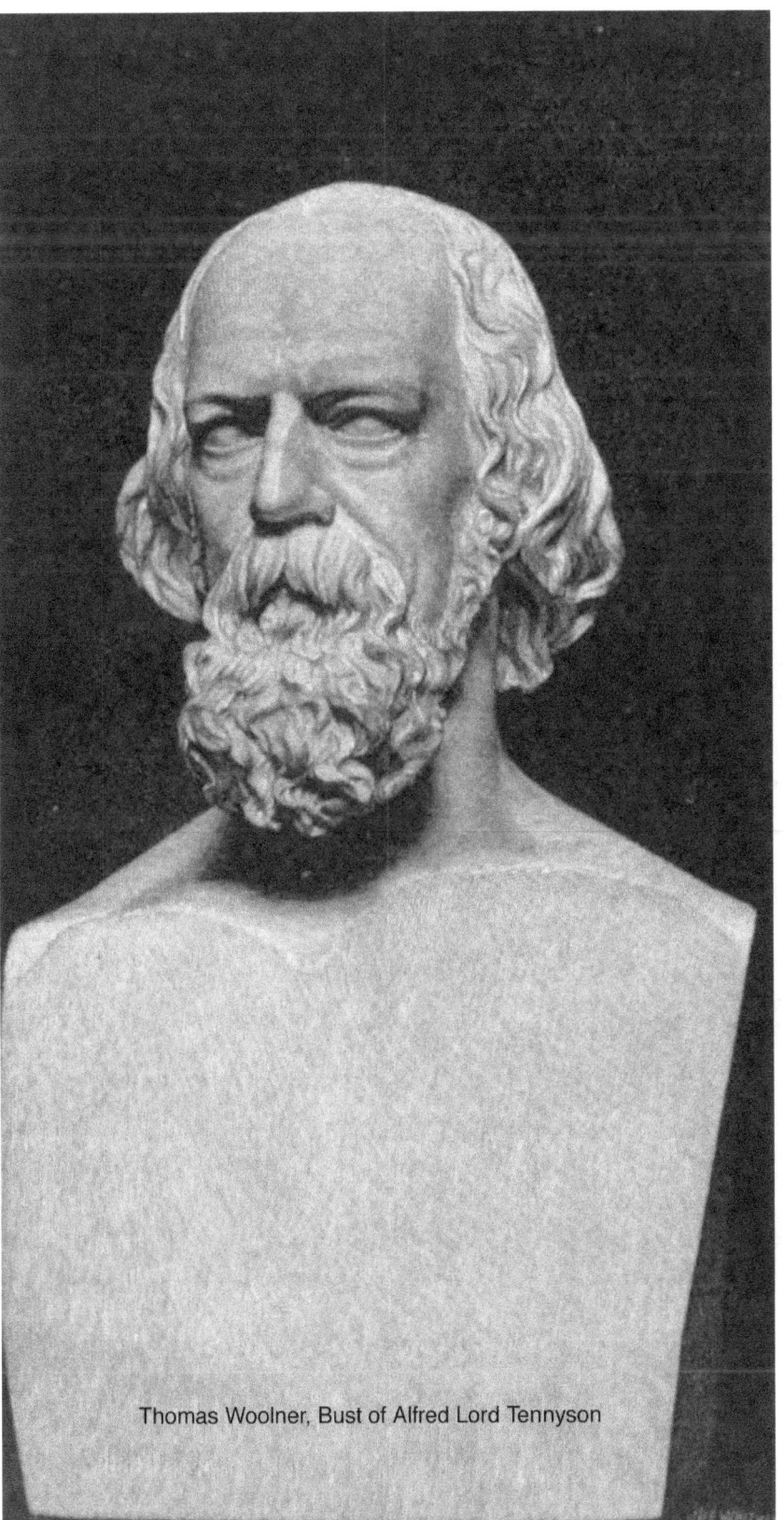
Thomas Woolner, Bust of Alfred Lord Tennyson

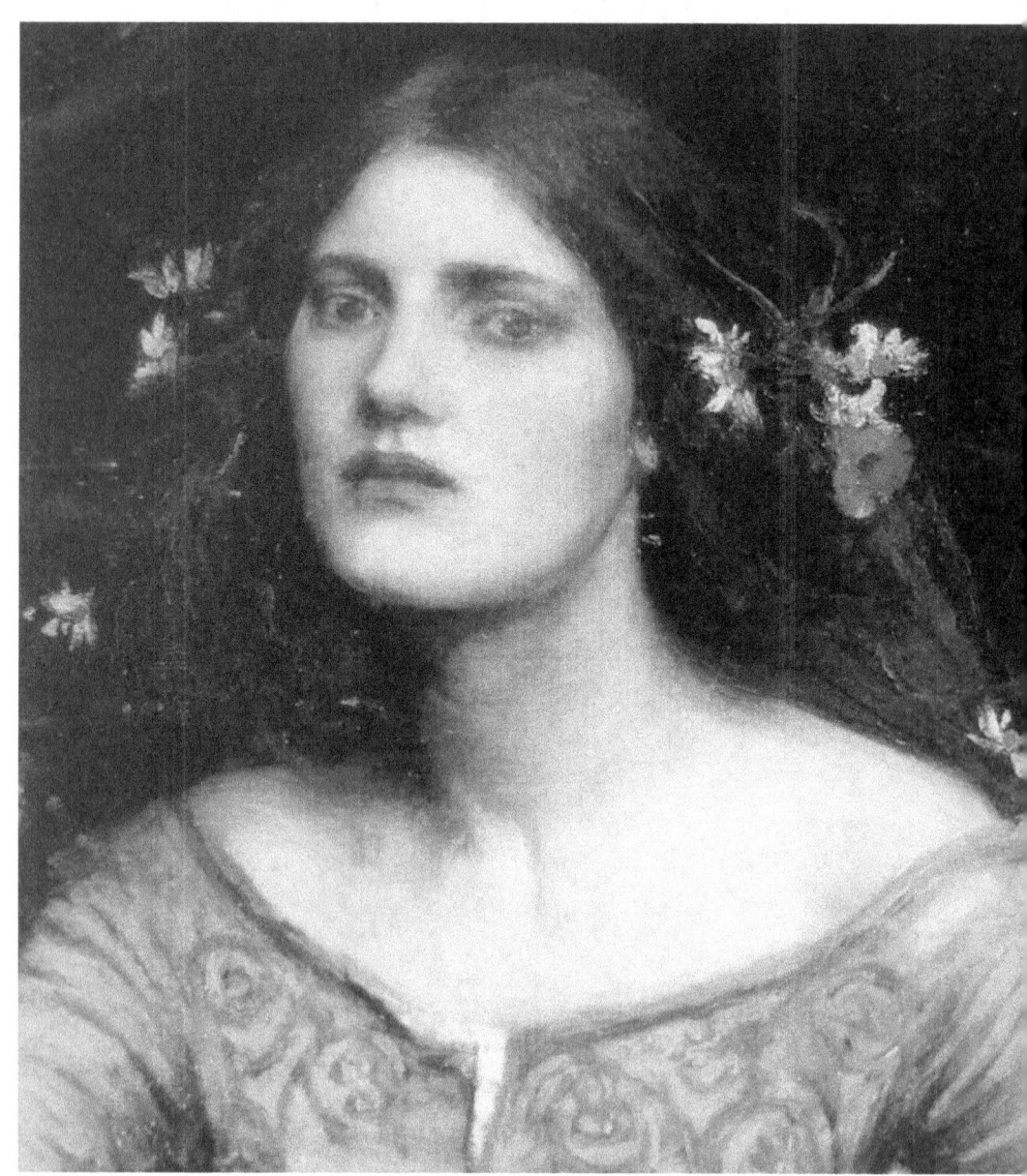

John William Waterhouse, Ophelia, 1910, detail

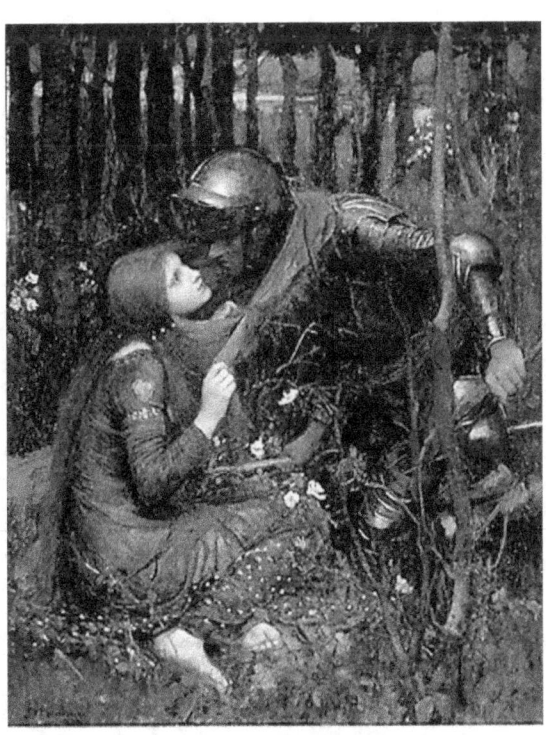

John Waterhouse, 'La Belle Dame Sans Merci'

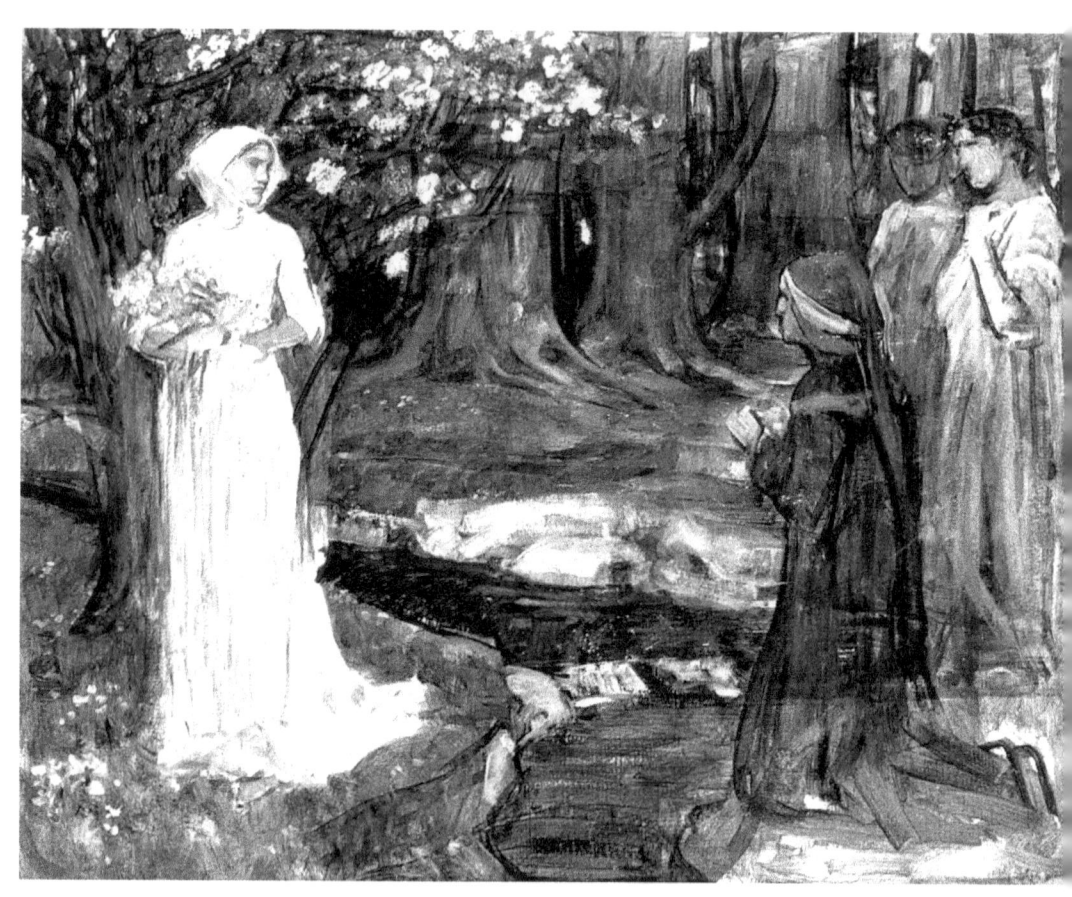

John William Waterhouse, Dante and Matilda, 1915,
Dahesh Museum of Art

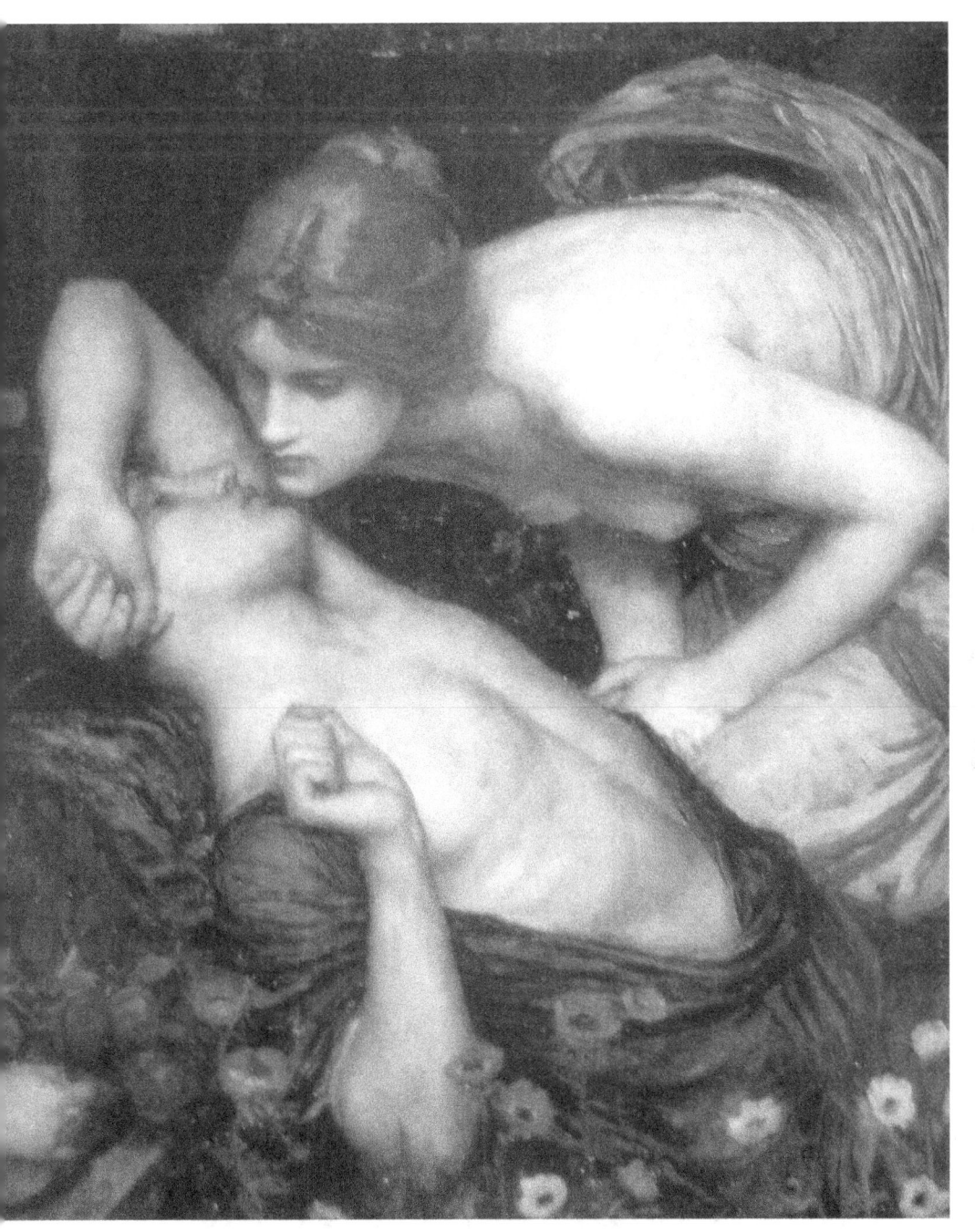

John William Waterhouse, The Awakening of Adonis, 1899, detail

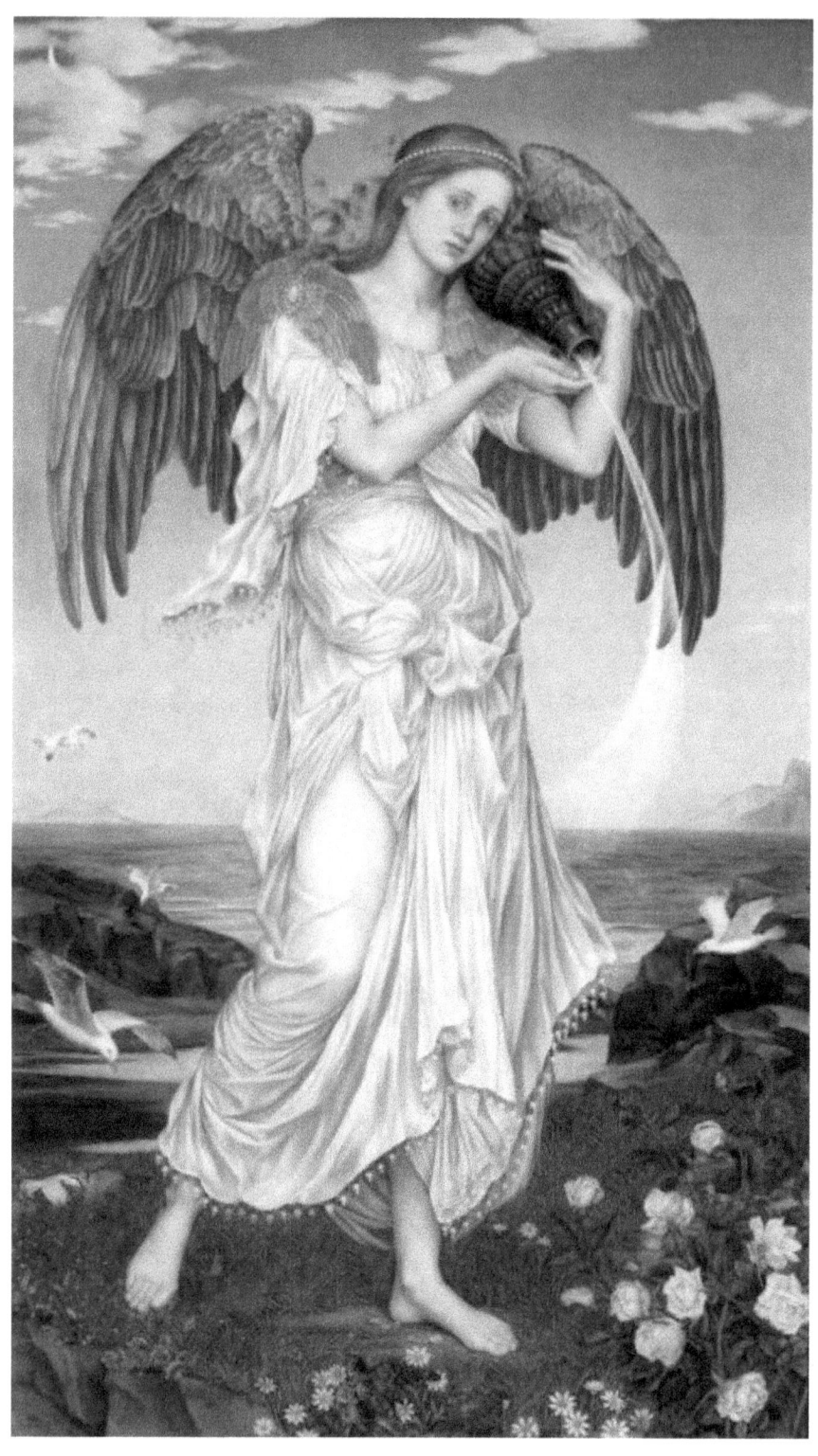

Evelyn de Morgan, Eos, 1895, Columbus, Ohio

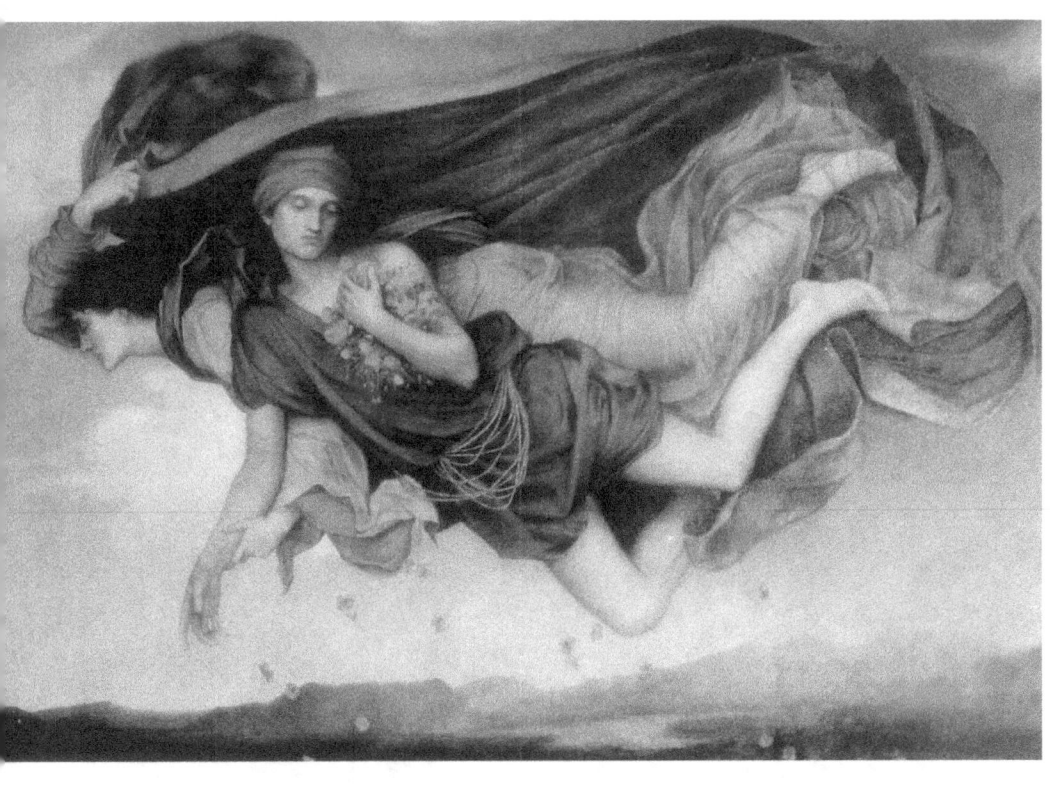

Evelyn de Morgan, Night and Sleep, 1878, Guildford

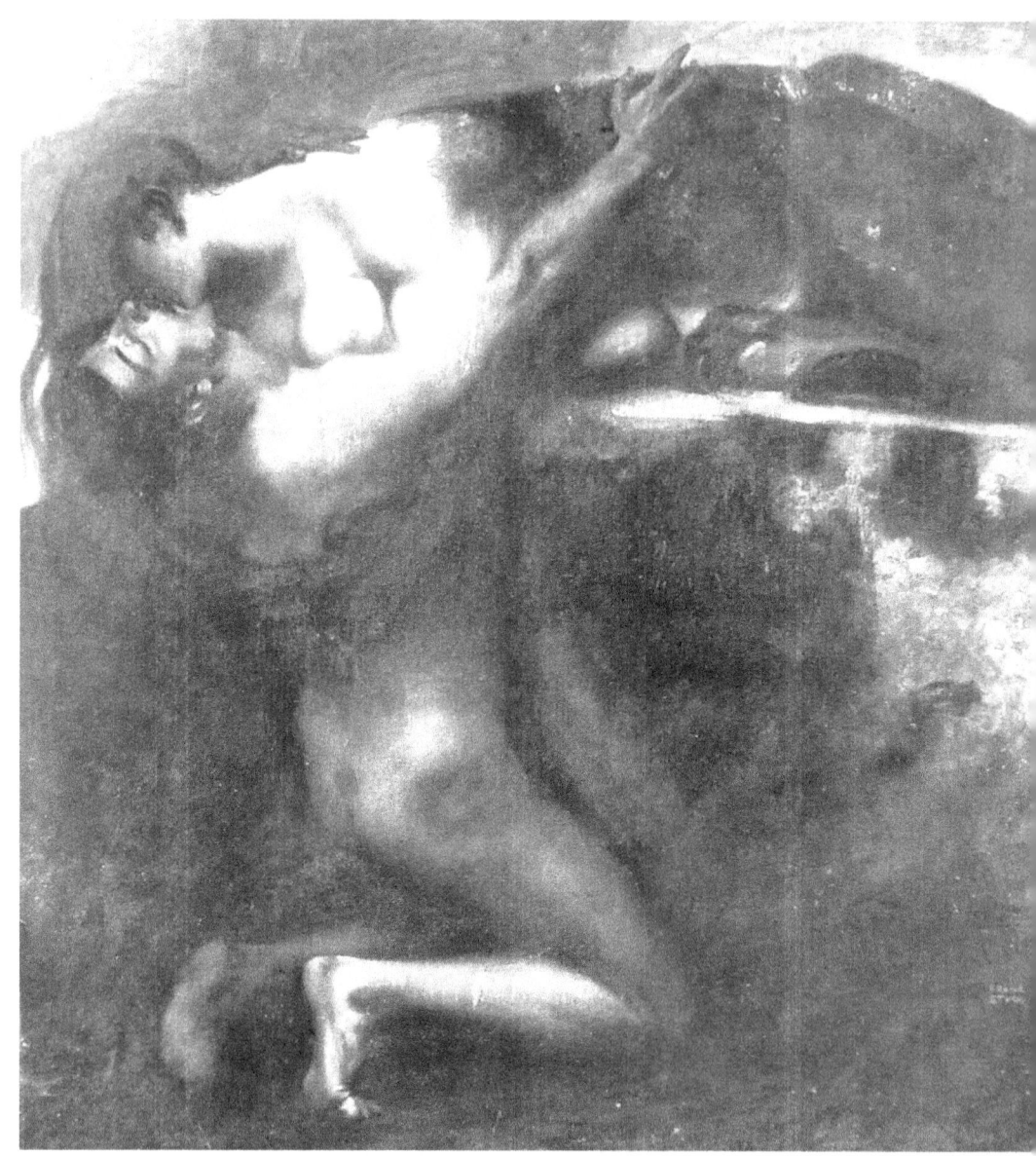

Franz von Stuck, Sphinx

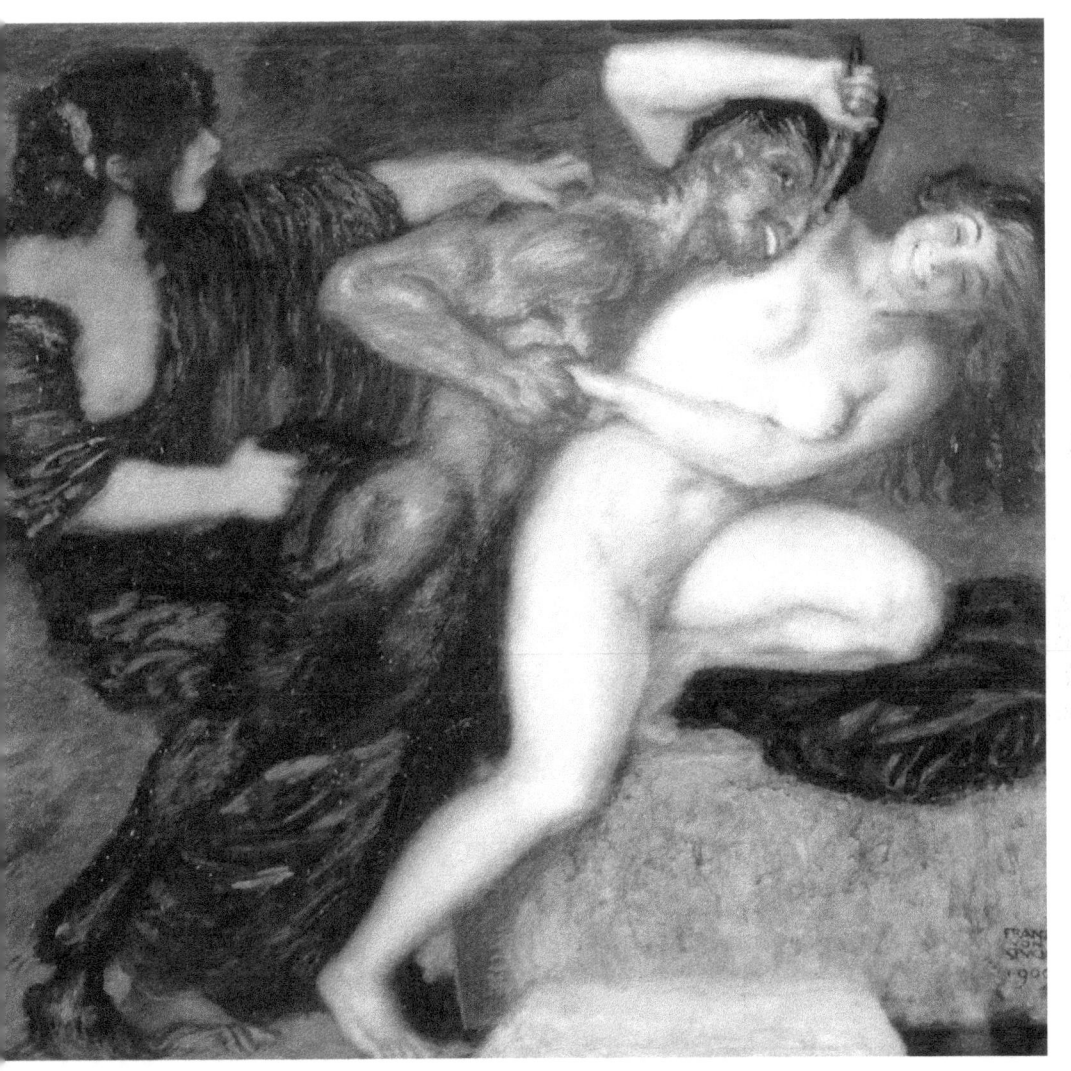

Franz von Stuck, Scherzo

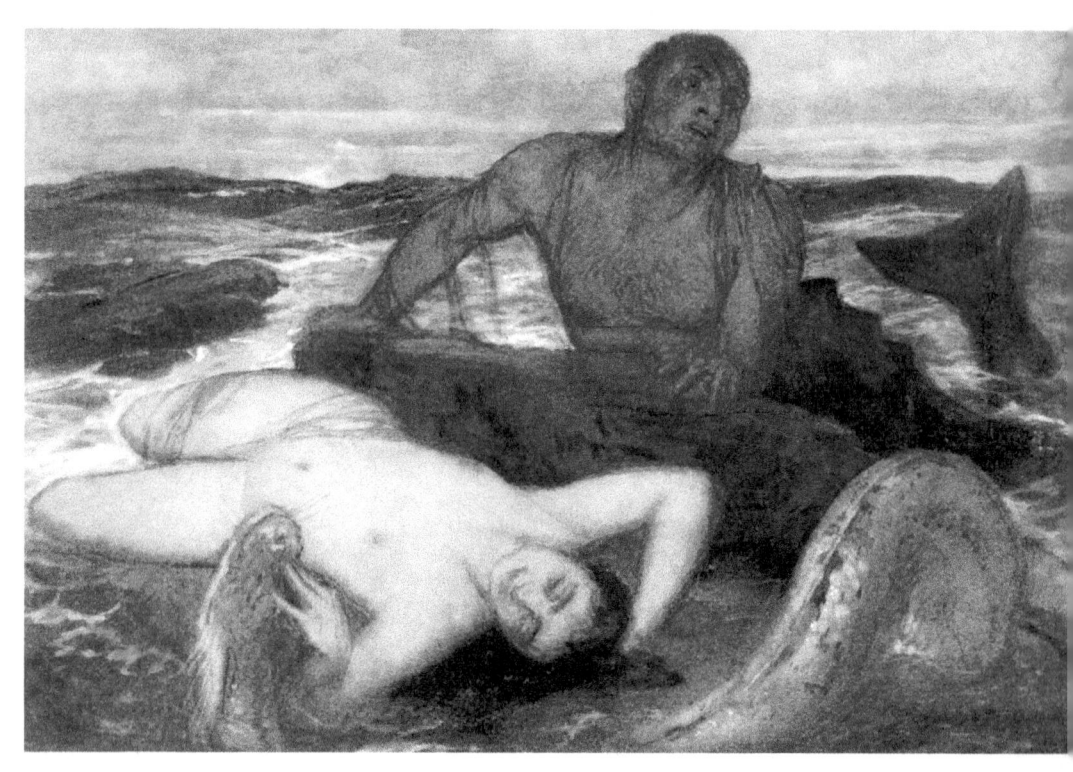

Arnold Böcklin, Triton and Nereid, 1877

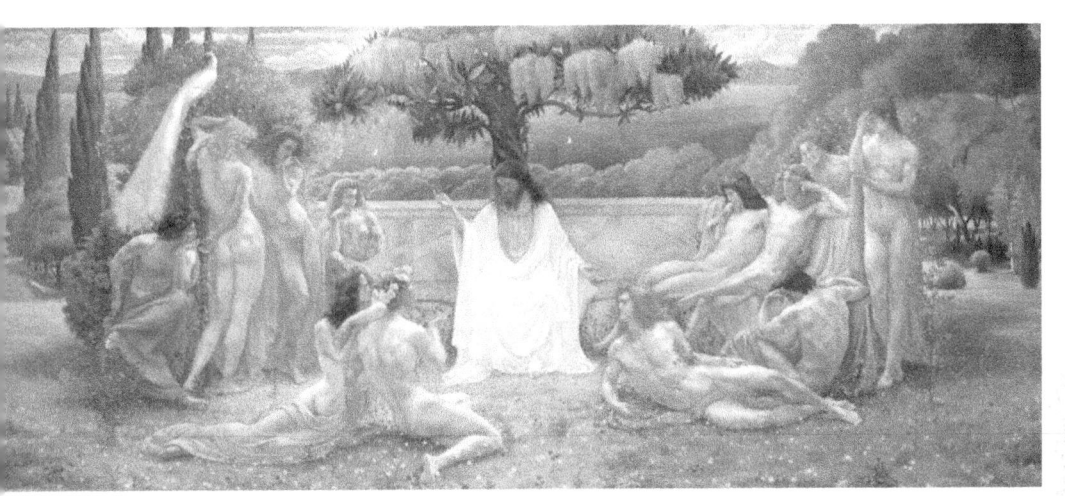

Jean Delville, The School of Plato, 1898

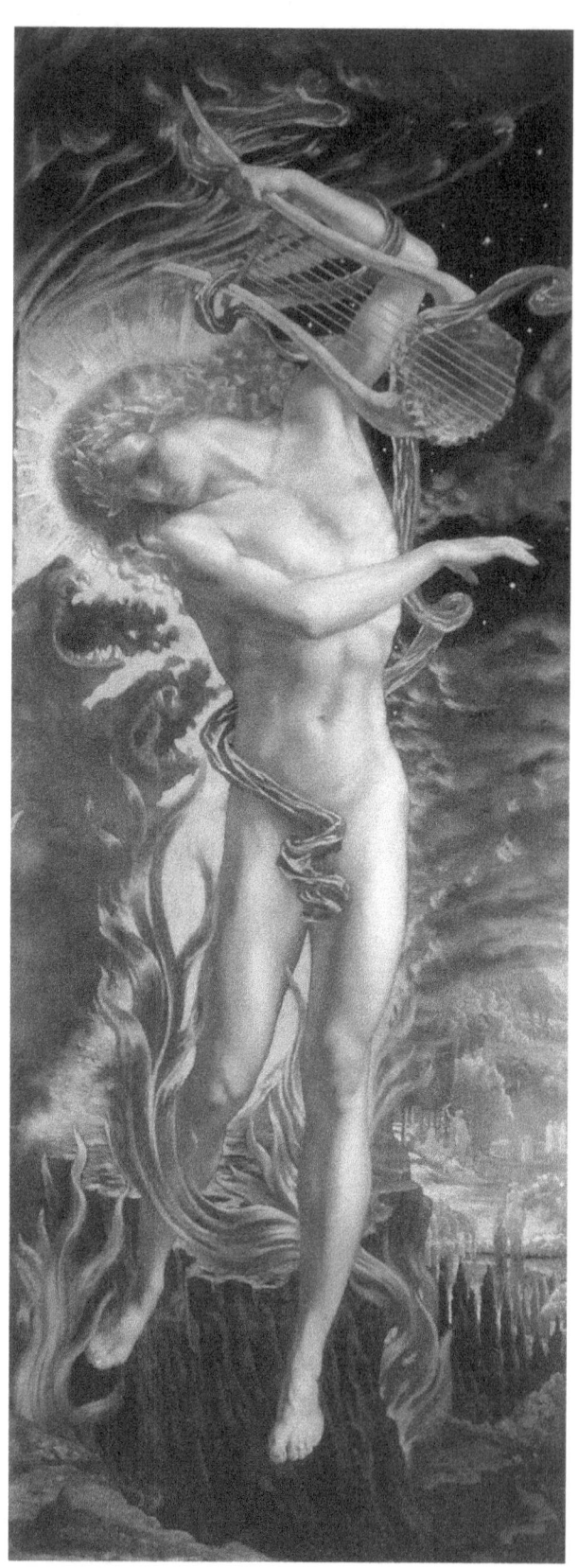

Jean Delville,
Orpheus,
late 19th century

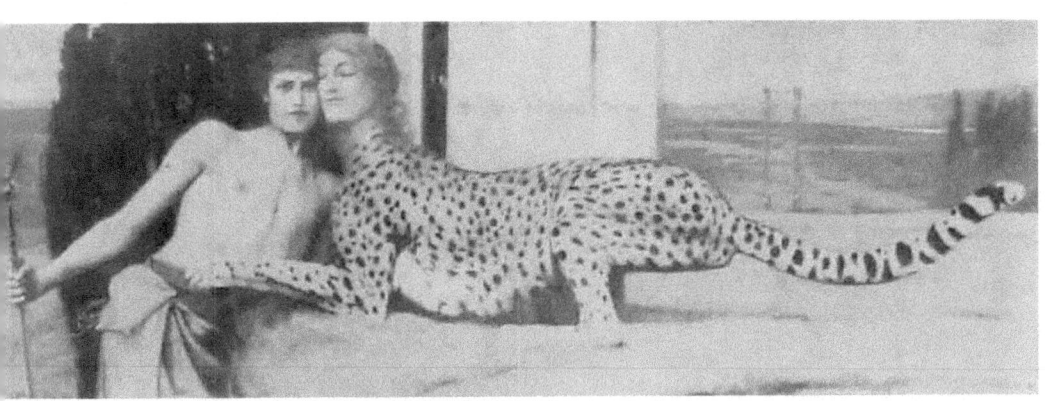

Fernand Knopff, The Caresses of the Sphinx, 1896, Brussels

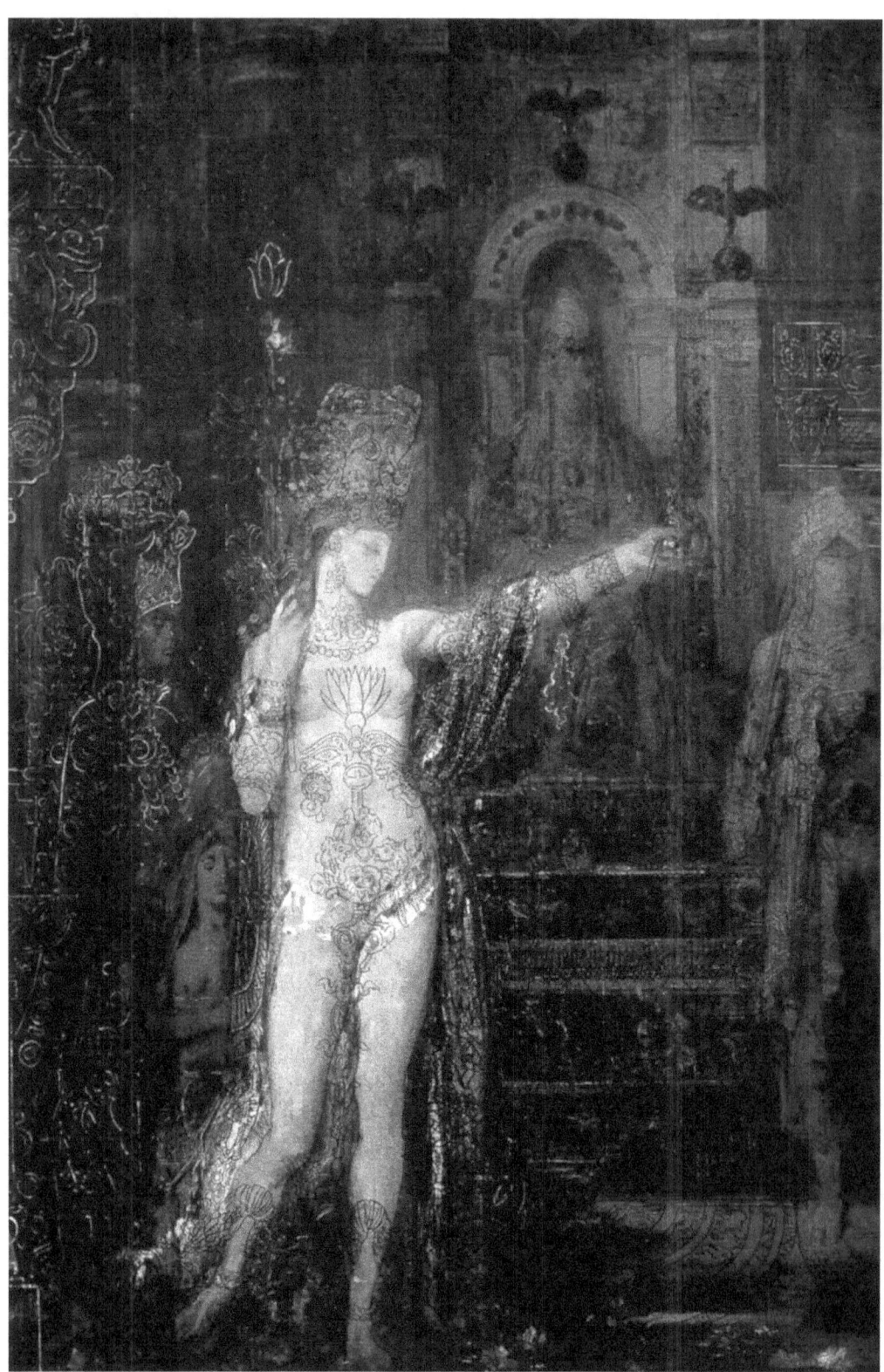

Gustave Moreau, Salomé, 1876

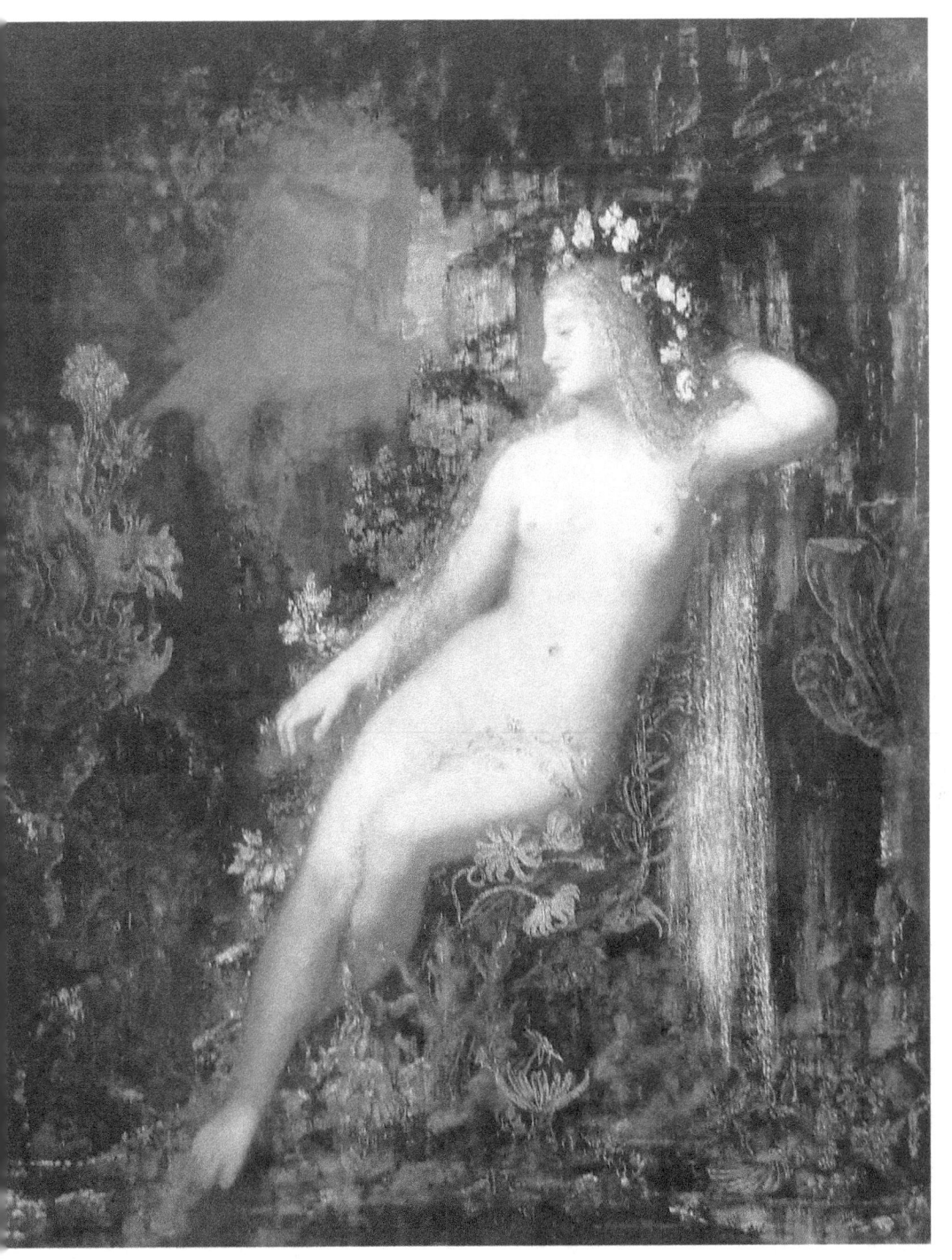

Gustave Moreau, Galatea, 1880

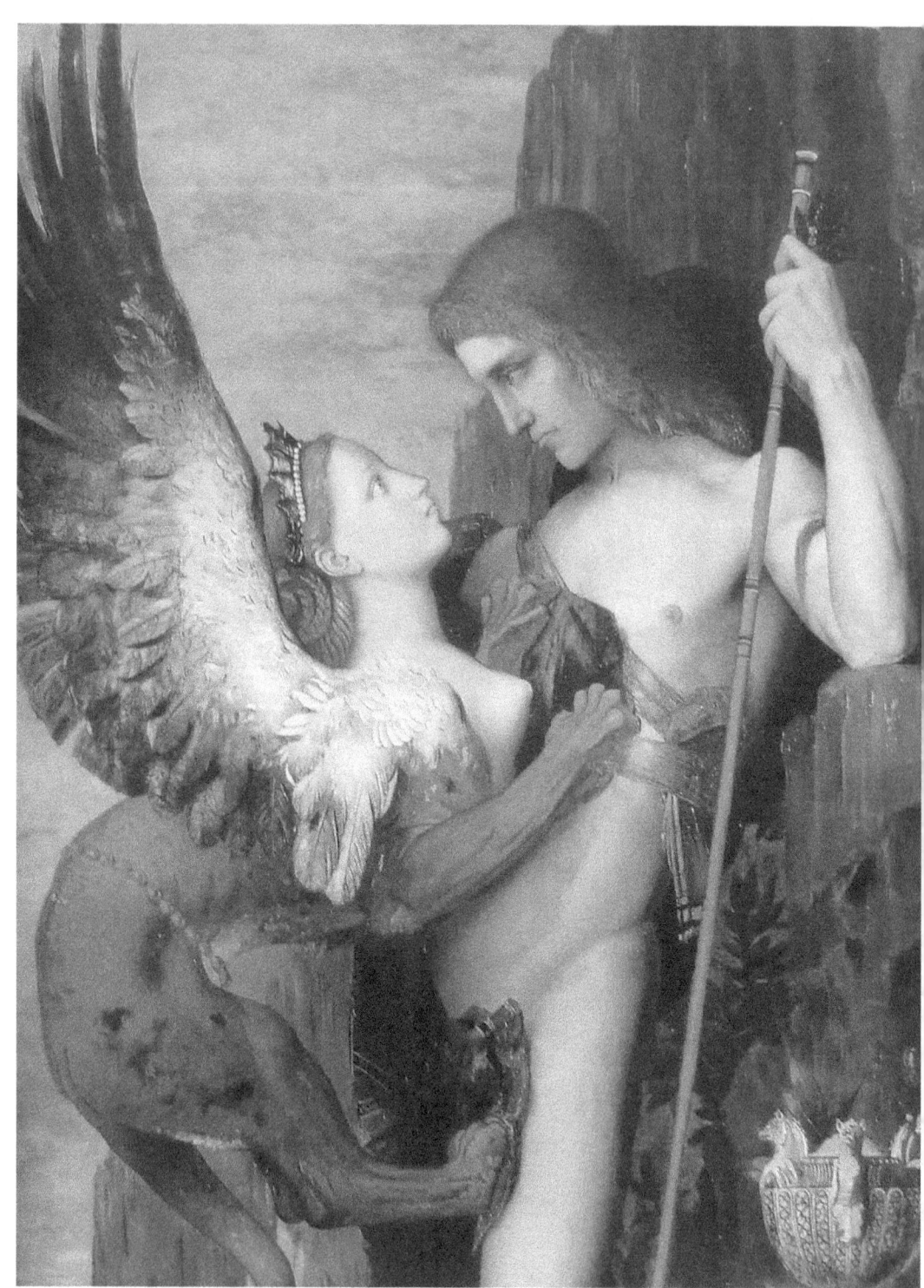

Gustave Moreau, The Sphinx

CRESCENT MOON PUBLISHING

web: www.crmoon.com e-mail: cresmopub@yahoo.co.uk

ARTS, PAINTING, SCULPTURE

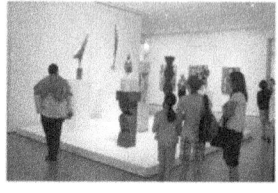
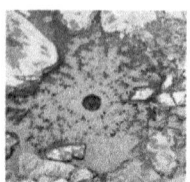
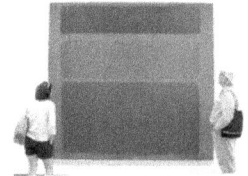

The Art of Andy Goldsworthy
Andy Goldsworthy: Touching Nature
Andy Goldsworthy in Close-Up
Andy Goldsworthy: Pocket Guide
Andy Goldsworthy In America
Land Art: A Complete Guide
The Art of Richard Long
Richard Long: Pocket Guide
Land Art In the UK
Land Art in Close-Up
Land Art In the U.S.A.
Land Art: Pocket Guide
Installation Art in Close-Up
Minimal Art and Artists In the 1960s and After
Colourfield Painting
Land Art DVD, TV documentary
Andy Goldsworthy DVD, TV documentary
The Erotic Object: Sexuality in Sculpture From Prehistory to the Present Day
Sex in Art: Pornography and Pleasure in Painting and Sculpture
Postwar Art
Sacred Gardens: The Garden in Myth, Religion and Art
Glorification: Religious Abstraction in Renaissance and 20th Century Art
Early Netherlandish Painting
Leonardo da Vinci
Piero della Francesca
Giovanni Bellini
Fra Angelico: Art and Religion in the Renaissance
Mark Rothko: The Art of Transcendence
Frank Stella: American Abstract Artist
Jasper Johns
Brice Marden
Alison Wilding: The Embrace of Sculpture
Vincent van Gogh: Visionary Landscapes
Eric Gill: Nuptials of God
Constantin Brancusi: Sculpting the Essence of Things
Max Beckmann
Caravaggio
Gustave Moreau
Egon Schiele: Sex and Death In Purple Stockings
Delizioso Fotografico Fervore: Works In Process 1
Sacro Cuore: Works In Process 2
The Light Eternal: J.M.W. Turner
The Madonna Glorified: Karen Arthurs

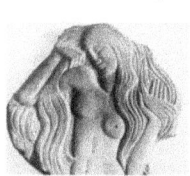
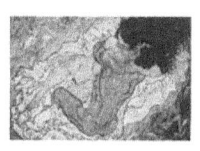
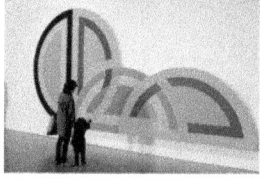
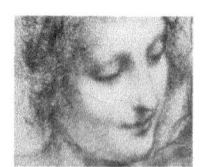
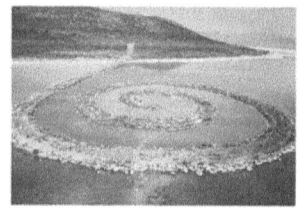

LITERATURE

J.R.R. Tolkien: The Books, The Films, The Whole Cultural Phenomenon
J.R.R. Tolkien: Pocket Guide
Tolkien's Heroic Quest
The *Earthsea* Books of Ursula Le Guin
Beauties, Beasts and Enchantment: Classic French Fairy Tales
German Popular Stories by the Brothers Grimm
Philip Pullman and *His Dark Materials*
Sexing Hardy: Thomas Hardy and Feminism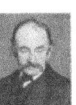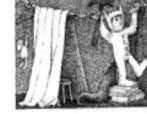
Thomas Hardy's *Tess of the d'Urbervilles*
Thomas Hardy's *Jude the Obscure*
Thomas Hardy: The Tragic Novels
Love and Tragedy: Thomas Hardy
The Poetry of Landscape in Hardy
Wessex Revisited: Thomas Hardy and John Cowper Powys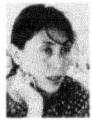
Wolfgang Iser: Essays and Interviews
Petrarch, Dante and the Troubadours
Maurice Sendak and the Art of Children's Book Illustration
Andrea Dworkin
Cixous, Irigaray, Kristeva: The *Jouissance* of French Feminism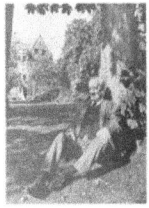
Julia Kristeva: Art, Love, Melancholy, Philosophy, Semiotics and Psychoanalysis
Hélène Cixous I Love You: The *Jouissance* of Writing
Luce Irigaray: Lips, Kissing, and the Politics of Sexual Difference
Peter Redgrove: Here Comes the Flood
Peter Redgrove: Sex-Magic-Poetry-Cornwall
Lawrence Durrell: Between Love and Death, East and West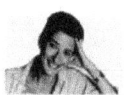
Love, Culture & Poetry: Lawrence Durrell
Cavafy: Anatomy of a Soul
German Romantic Poetry: Goethe, Novalis, Heine, Hölderlin
Feminism and Shakespeare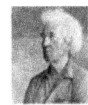
Shakespeare: Love, Poetry & Magic
The Passion of D.H. Lawrence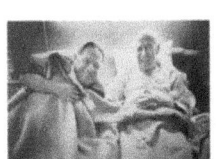
D.H. Lawrence: Symbolic Landscapes
D.H. Lawrence: Infinite Sensual Violence
Rimbaud: Arthur Rimbaud and the Magic of Poetry
The Ecstasies of John Cowper Powys
Sensualism and Mythology: The Wessex Novels of John Cowper Powys
Amorous Life: John Cowper Powys and the Manifestation of Affectivity (H.W. Fawkner)
Postmodern Powys: New Essays on John Cowper Powys (Joe Boulter)
Rethinking Powys: Critical Essays on John Cowper Powys
Paul Bowles & Bernardo Bertolucci
Rainer Maria Rilke
Joseph Conrad: *Heart of Darkness*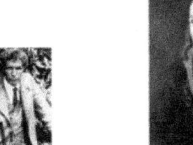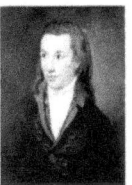
In the Dim Void: Samuel Beckett
Samuel Beckett Goes into the Silence
André Gide: Fiction and Fervour
Jackie Collins and the Blockbuster Novel
Blinded By Her Light: The Love-Poetry of Robert Graves
The Passion of Colours: Travels In Mediterranean Lands
Poetic Forms

POETRY

Ursula Le Guin: Walking In Cornwall
Peter Redgrove: Here Comes The Flood
Peter Redgrove: Sex-Magic-Poetry-Cornwall
Dante: Selections From the Vita Nuova
Petrarch, Dante and the Troubadours
William Shakespeare: Sonnets
William Shakespeare: Complete Poems
Blinded By Her Light: The Love-Poetry of Robert Graves
Emily Dickinson: Selected Poems
Emily Brontë: Poems
Thomas Hardy: Selected Poems
Percy Bysshe Shelley: Poems
John Keats: Selected Poems
Joh n Keats: Poems of 1820
D.H. Lawrence: Selected Poems
Edmund Spenser: Poems
Edmund Spenser: Amoretti
John Donne: Poems
Henry Vaughan: Poems
Sir Thomas Wyatt: Poems
Robert Herrick: Selected Poems
Rilke: Space, Essence and Angels in the Poetry of Rainer Maria Rilke
Rainer Maria Rilke: Selected Poems
Friedrich Hölderlin: Selected Poems
Arseny Tarkovsky: Selected Poems
Arthur Rimbaud: Selected Poems
Arthur Rimbaud: A Season in Hell
Arthur Rimbaud and the Magic of Poetry
Novalis: Hymns To the Night
German Romantic Poetry
Paul Verlaine: Selected Poems
Elizaethan Sonnet Cycles
D.J. Enright: By-Blows
Jeremy Reed: Brigitte's Blue Heart
Jeremy Reed: Claudia Schiffer's Red Shoes
Gorgeous Little Orpheus
Radiance: New Poems
Crescent Moon Book of Nature Poetry
Crescent Moon Book of Love Poetry
Crescent Moon Book of Mystical Poetry
Crescent Moon Book of Elizabethan Love Poetry
Crescent Moon Book of Metaphysical Poetry
Crescent Moon Book of Romantic Poetry
Pagan America: New American Poetry

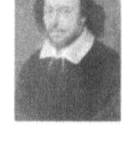
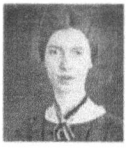
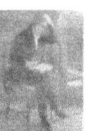
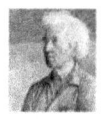
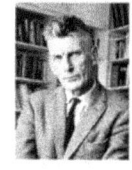
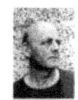
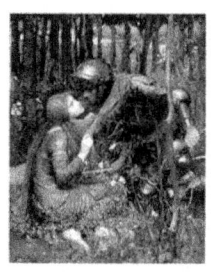
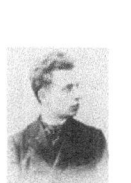
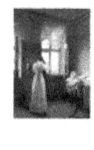
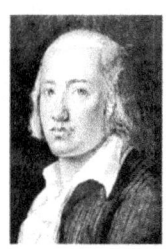
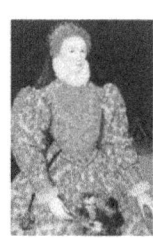

MEDIA, CINEMA, FEMINISM and CULTURAL STUDIES

J.R.R. Tolkien: The Books, The Films, The Whole Cultural Phenomenon
J.R.R. Tolkien: Pocket Guide
The *Lord of the Rings* Movies: Pocket Guide
The Cinema of Hayao Miyazaki
Hayao Miyazaki: *Princess Mononoke*: Pocket Movie Guide
Hayao Miyazaki: *Spirited Away*: Pocket Movie Guide
Tim Burton : Hallowe'en For Hollywood
Ken Russell
Ken Russell: *Tommy*: Pocket Movie Guide
The Ghost Dance: The Origins of Religion
The Peyote Cult
Cixous, Irigaray, Kristeva: The *Jouissance* of French Feminism
Julia Kristeva: Art, Love, Melancholy, Philosophy, Semiotics and Psychoanalysis
Luce Irigaray: Lips, Kissing, and the Politics of Sexual Difference
Hélene Cixous I Love You: The *Jouissance* of Writing
Andrea Dworkin
'Cosmo Woman': The World of Women's Magazines
Women in Pop Music
HomeGround: The Kate Bush Anthology
Discovering the Goddess (Geoffrey Ashe)
The Poetry of Cinema
The Sacred Cinema of Andrei Tarkovsky
Andrei Tarkovsky: Pocket Guide
Andrei Tarkovsky: *Mirror*: Pocket Movie Guide
Andrei Tarkovsky: *The Sacrifice*: Pocket Movie Guide
Walerian Borowczyk: Cinema of Erotic Dreams
Jean-Luc Godard: The Passion of Cinema
Jean-Luc Godard: *Hail Mary*: Pocket Movie Guide
Jean-Luc Godard: *Contempt*: Pocket Movie Guide
Jean-Luc Godard: *Pierrot le Fou*: Pocket Movie Guide
John Hughes and Eighties Cinema
Ferris Bueller's Day Off: Pocket Movie Guide
Jean-Luc Godard: Pocket Guide
The Cinema of Richard Linklater
Liv Tyler: Star In Ascendance
Blade Runner and the Films of Philip K. Dick
Paul Bowles and Bernardo Bertolucci
Media Hell: Radio, TV and the Press
An Open Letter to the BBC
Detonation Britain: Nuclear War in the UK
Feminism and Shakespeare
Wild Zones: Pornography, Art and Feminism
Sex in Art: Pornography and Pleasure in Painting and Sculpture
Sexing Hardy: Thomas Hardy and Feminism

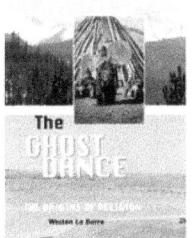
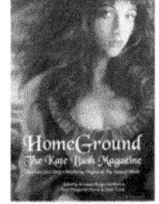
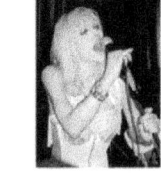
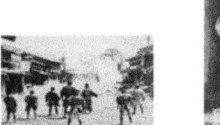
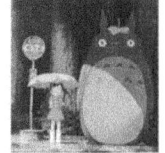
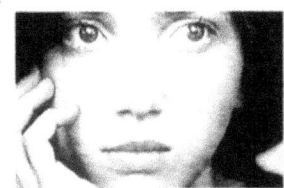

The Light Eternal is a model monograph, an exemplary job. The subject matter of the book is beautifully organised and dead on beam. (Lawrence Durrell)
It is amazing for me to see my work treated with such passion and respect. (Andrea Dworkin)

CRESCENT MOON PUBLISHING
P.O. Box 1312, Maidstone, Kent, ME14 5XU, Great Britain. www.crmoon.com

cresmopub@yahoo.co.uk   www.crescentmoon.org.uk

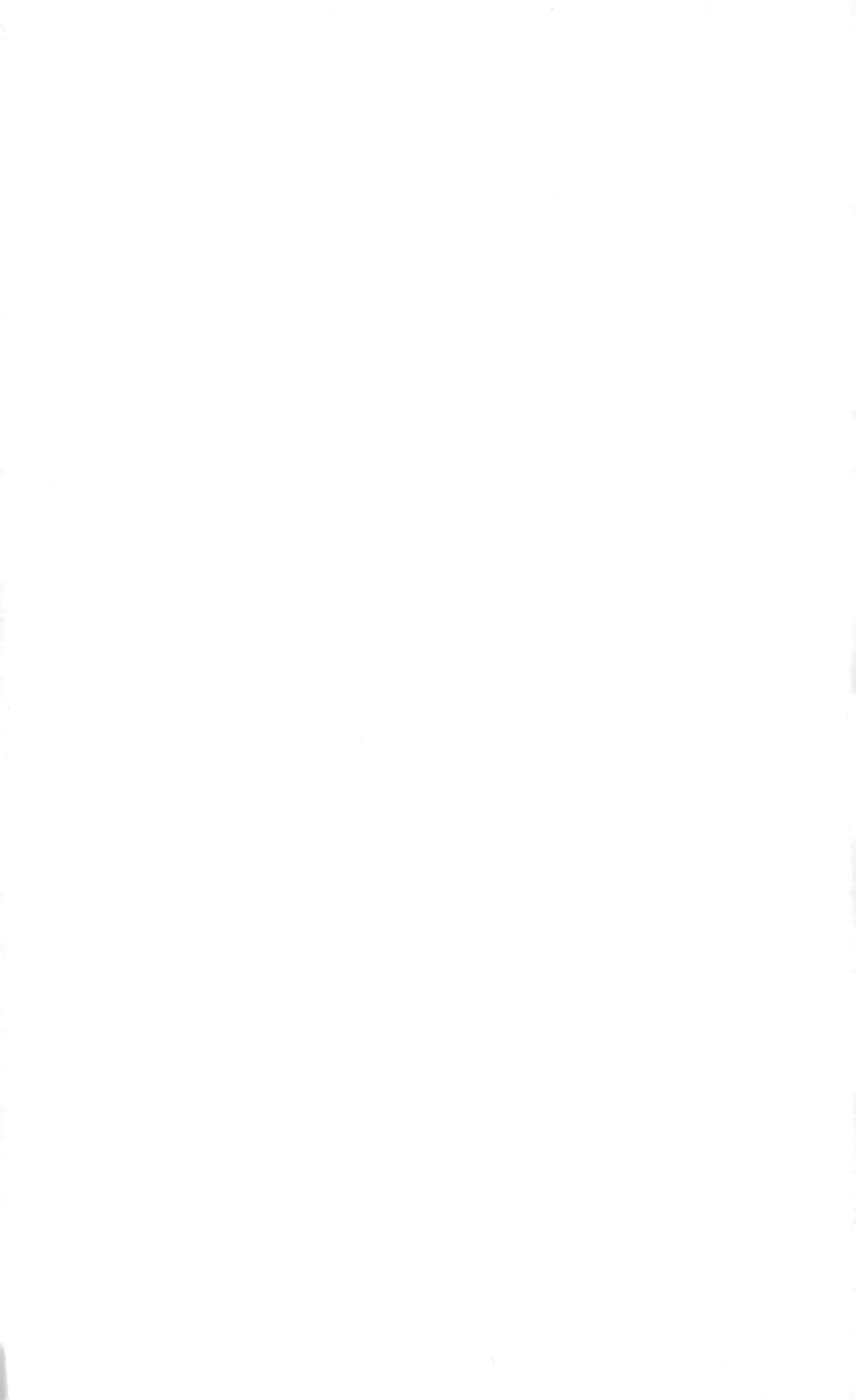